Responsive Mentoring

Responsive Mentoring

Supporting the Teachers All Students Deserve

Wendy Gardiner
Nina F. Weisling

ROWMAN & LITTLEFIELD
Lanham • Boulder • New York • London

Published by Rowman & Littlefield
An imprint of The Rowman & Littlefield Publishing Group, Inc.
4501 Forbes Boulevard, Suite 200, Lanham, Maryland 20706
www.rowman.com

6 Tinworth Street, London SE11 5AL, United Kingdom

British Library Cataloguing in Publication Information Available

Library of Congress Cataloging-in-Publication Data

Names: Gardiner, Wendy, 1967– author. | Weisling, Nina F., 1980– author.
Title: Responsive mentoring : supporting the teachers all students deserve / Wendy Gardiner, Nina F. Weisling.
Description: Lanham : Rowman & Littlefield, [2020] | Includes bibliographical references. | Summary: "Responsive Mentoring advocates for an approach to mentoring that is teacher-centered, scaffolded, and contextualized to teachers' work."—Provided by publisher.
Identifiers: LCCN 2020006327 (print) | LCCN 2020006328 (ebook) | ISBN 9781475851366 (cloth) | ISBN 9781475851373 (paperback) | ISBN 9781475851380 (epub)
Subjects: LCSH: Mentoring in education. | Teacher effectiveness. | Interpersonal relations.
Classification: LCC LB1731.4 .G39 2020 (print) | LCC LB1731.4 (ebook) | DDC 371.102—dc23
LC record available at https://lccn.loc.gov/2020006327
LC ebook record available at https://lccn.loc.gov/2020006328

To the mentors and teachers who opened their classrooms to us,
to the many mentors who have guided us through our careers,
and to our families and colleagues who supported us in writing this book.
We are grateful to you all.

Contents

Foreword

If *Responsive Mentoring: Supporting the Teachers All Students Deserve* caught your attention, chances are that we share something important in common with authors—and that is a steadfast belief that the work of mentoring other teachers, in all stages from aspiring through deeply experienced, requires expertise beyond being an "effective" teacher. For me, that daunting realization came when I was just three years into my teaching career and on the cusp of starting graduate school—long before I ever entered academia and embarked upon my own research into teacher preparation. My principal asked me to serve as a mentor to a student teacher I'll call Kerry. Brimming with verve and lofty aspirations, I threw myself into my new responsibility. Like so many in the role, I relied heavily on my own "apprenticeship of observation" in mentoring and mimicked the moves that my wonderful mentor teacher used with me just a few years earlier. Kerry was struggling to plan substantive lessons for my eager fourth and fifth graders. Although I tried my best to provide her with encouragement and curricular resources, it quickly became clear to me that I did not have additional concrete models to support her learning.

My younger self would have greatly benefited from an insightful, practical guide to mentorship like the one before you. Wendy Gardiner and Nina F. Weisling have drawn upon their years of experience both as educators and as researchers to create an inviting text that recognizes mentorship for the complex practice that it is. Of importance is their insistence that excellent teachers—and the mentors who shape them—are *made*, not born. In other words, mentoring can and should be taught intentionally and explicitly. Instead, educators too often rely on the pervasive but mistaken idea—as I once did—that those who can teach will naturally know how to mentor other teachers.

Gardiner and Weisling dismantle that widespread falsehood and present a variety of research-based ideas that mentors across the continuum can immediately implement to improve the gamut, from aspiring teachers to those who work alongside and coach their peers, and from first-timers to those who have been mentoring for years. In these pages, you'll learn not only how to mentor more effectively but also how to support the professional training and development of mentors themselves, an often-overlooked area.

Their work draws heavily upon the concept of educative mentoring, a collaborative framework given to us by the ultimate mentor, Sharon Feiman-Nemser. They build on Feiman-Nemser's concept of educative mentoring, which calls for taking an inquiry-based stance toward teacher learning and for treating mentoring as a professional practice. They provide authentic reflections on mentoring and teacher learning by many real-world educators. Gardiner and Weisling engage and support the reader by providing reflection questions throughout, which can ultimately inspire meaningful action and important steps toward learning.

In my first experience as a mentor, things did not go as smoothly as I had hoped, and for a variety of reasons, Kerry did not proceed with her certification program. To this day, I cannot help but wonder if her path would have been different had I been a more informed mentor teacher. (Kerry, if you are out there, I'm sorry I did not know better, and I trust you've landed in the right place for you!). My experience with my first student teacher left me with the enduring lesson that mentoring should be treated with the respect and rigor it deserves.

For years, the literature has spoken to the importance of mentoring, especially for in-service teachers and more recently for preservice teachers, but very few have spoken to *how*. *Responsive Mentoring: Supporting the Teachers All Students Deserve* provides us with practical ways to enact the how. After all, no less is at stake than the development and retention of the next generation of educators, who will go on to make a real difference in the lives of our students.

Kavita Kapadia Matsko
Associate Professor/Associate Dean for Teacher Education
School of Education and Social Policy
Northwestern University, Evanston, Illinois

Preface

When we first met more than 10 years ago, Wendy was an assistant professor in Chicago, working directly with preservice and practicing elementary literacy teachers. Through this work, Wendy supported mentors' professional development and conducted research on induction mentoring. At the same time, Nina was finishing her doctorate in special education and co-leading a mentoring program of 25 mentors across 33 Chicago Public Schools.

These collective experiences, along with our combined 24 years of prior work as classroom teachers and mentors, surfaced our shared core beliefs that *all* students deserve highly effective educators and that to be an effective educator requires ongoing, intentional, ambitious, and responsive support. Given the promise and prominence of mentoring to support teachers, together we set out to learn more about how new mentors develop their identities and practice, and how veteran mentors make decisions about which practices to use as well as when, how, and why.

Our work in classrooms and with students, coupled with our collaborative research, revealed much about what it is to mentor. Mentoring is deceptively complex, mentally taxing, and highly rewarding work (as any mentors reading this book already know!). We quickly realized that not every mentor had access to mentor-specific professional development. Even for those who are part of well-established programs, systematized training and substantive professional development is frequently absent (Aspfors & Fransson, 2015). We hope that writing this book contributes to closing this gap.

More specifically, our goals in writing this book were threefold: (1) to expand and amplify the vision of mentoring as responsive, instructionally oriented, and teacher centered; (2) to offer a shared vision of *educative mentoring* and to add clarity on ways educative mentoring can responsively occur in practice (Feiman-Nemser, 2012; Schwille, 2008); and (3) to provide concrete and actionable strategies for mentors' professional growth and on-going support. In short, we firmly believe that the content in this book can increase mentors' knowledge, efficacy, and satisfaction, and as a result, make a positive impact on teachers' and students' learning.

This book was a fully collaborative effort between both of us—we shared responsibility at every phase in its creation. We are both heavily indebted to the mentors and teachers who opened their classrooms and shared their experiences with us, to those who read drafts of our manuscript and gave us critical feedback to make it more useful to mentors, and to our publisher, for believing that a book about supporting mentors was an important investment. We are also thankful for the family and friends who supported us through the processes involved in writing and publishing.

In many ways, we wrote the book we wished we had when we were mentoring and leading mentor development. Through real-world examples, resources, and questions for reflection and action, we hope that mentors in *any* context and at *any* point in their career find relevant and meaningful opportunities to grow in their practice. The idea is not to prescribe but to build a rich foundation for mentoring and the flexible practices that mentors across experience levels can draw upon to support their efforts in this important work.

Introduction

Mentoring is complex and important work that can have long-lasting impact on teacher *and* student learning. Mentors can help teachers navigate the many challenges of entering into and growing within the teaching profession. Mentors can help new and veteran teachers expand their knowledge base and implement ambitious, equitable instruction with all students. Mentors can help teachers develop as reflective practitioners who learn in and from teaching. As a result, mentors can also have a significant impact not only on teacher learning but also on students' learning and their development of positive academic identities.

With all the promise and possibilities of mentoring, it should be no surprise that over the past 20 years there has been a vast increase in the number of mentoring programs offered and the number of teachers becoming mentors. To support this important work, books have been written, workshops and conferences have been offered, and more.

At the same time, some troubling patterns have emerged that inhibit mentors and mentoring programs from meeting the aim of developing knowledgeable, reflective professionals who enact ambitious, responsive, and equitable instruction for all students. Chief among those is the assumption that effective teachers will automatically become effective mentors.

The reality is that mentoring and teaching require different skill sets. Therefore, mentors need intentional support in developing, applying, and evaluating mentoring skills. Unfortunately, for mentors, teachers, and students alike, mentors do not always receive the depth and breadth of professional learning needed to make them as impactful as they could be. Further complicating the field of mentoring, and relatedly the development of mentors, is the range of sometimes-competing beliefs on what purposes mentoring should serve and how mentoring should be enacted to meet those aims.

Throughout this book, we respond to the challenges we see by providing a clear vision of mentoring around which mentors and teachers can focus their work. To help mentors translate this vision into an effective and responsive practice, we describe a set of mentoring practices for mentors to use flexibly and in collaboration with teachers. We also provide advice on how to mentor *mentors* to ensure they are prepared to be responsive in their work with teachers, as well as supported to grow as professionals themselves.

Throughout this book, the term *mentor* is used to refer to educators with specialized knowledge who have a formal role in the professional development of preservice, new, and experienced teachers. Other programs may use *coach*, *mentor teacher*, or *supervisor* to reflect similar roles and responsibilities. This book was written thinking broadly about who mentors and in what circumstances mentoring occurs, including but not limited to

- new and more experienced mentors,
- mentors fully released from teaching responsibilities to work with new or experienced teachers,
- mentors who mentor while also teaching (not full release),
- instructional coaches who work to support teachers in single or multiple content areas, and
- teaching assistants or university supervisors who mentor preservice teachers.

A SHARED LANGUAGE AND FRAMEWORK

Across the field, there are many visions of what mentoring is, how mentoring should unfold, and what effective teaching and learning looks like. This book is grounded in Sharon Feiman-Nemser's (1998, 2001, 2012) work on *educative mentoring*. Educative mentoring is a collaborative, responsive, scaffolded framework aimed at fostering teachers' professional learning. Educative mentors help teachers identify *ambitious instructional goals* that meet the needs of all learners. Then, mentor and teacher work collaboratively to realize these goals.

This book draws from across the field of teacher education to describe *ambitious instruction* as

- responding to and drawing upon students' strengths, preferences, needs, and cultural assets when planning and teaching;
- holding high academic and learning expectations for all students;
- planning rigorous, standards-based instruction that embeds effective scaffolding;

- developing a classroom environment that stimulates curiosity, fosters intrinsic motivation and collaboration, and helps students persevere through challenges;
- engaging students actively and cognitively in their learning;
- eliciting and building off of students' thinking and orienting students to each other's thinking; and
- occurring in well-organized classrooms that have clear and shared routines and procedures that promote equitable learning and relationships among students.

Ambitious instruction reflects current standards for learning and occurs across all grades and content areas. Likewise, the mentoring vision and practices presented in this book support ambitious instruction across grade levels, content areas, and with new and experienced teachers.

To reflect this multidisciplinary approach toward supporting teachers, the term *instructional activities* (IAs) refers to the specific activities teachers engage in while implementing ambitious instruction. The term IA is used throughout the book liberally to encompass myriad activities, from routines and procedures to content-specific learning experiences. The shared characteristic is that IAs are intended to contribute to and facilitate equitable and ambitious learning opportunities.

Mentors have a unique capacity to work with teachers to set ambitious teaching and learning goals. Mentors can help teachers refine their goals and identify the related IAs they wish to implement and/or improve. From there, mentors collaborate with and scaffold teachers' development toward principled, independent practice.

The choice to use the gender-neutral *they* when referring to a singular teacher or mentor was deliberate and reflects a commitment to equitable practices. Direct quotes, as well as real examples from teachers, mentors, and classrooms, are used throughout. All names have been changed to preserve anonymity while ensuring the experiences are accurately described. This was done to protect and illustrate the hard work done by teachers and mentors together.

OVERVIEW OF THE BOOK

We broadly organize this book into three sections, each of which largely builds upon the previous sections and chapters: the foundations of effective mentoring (Chapters 1–3), practices mentors can employ in their work with teachers (Chapters 4–12), and methods for mentoring mentors (Chapters 13–16). Final thoughts are captured in the afterword.

Foundations of Effective Mentoring

In Chapter 1, we share our vision of mentoring—educative mentoring—a collaborative, responsive, scaffolded, and contextualized way of engaging with teachers to foster professional learning (cf. Feiman-Nemser, 1998, 2001, 2012). However, vision, while important, is not sufficient. Chapter 1 describes Schwille's (2008) temporal framework of *inside and outside mentoring practices* to provide mentors with a range of flexible practices to enact educative mentoring in truly responsive ways. *Inside* mentoring practices are used when students are present and the mentor is taking an active role in facilitating learning at that moment; *outside* mentoring practices take place before or after instruction occurs with the teacher's students. Inside and outside practices are used in many deliberate combinations, explored in further detail in Chapters 4–12.

Successful mentoring hinges on *trusting relationships* between and across invested stakeholders. Chapter 2 explains why trust—among mentor, teacher, administrators, and students—is the foundation upon which responsive mentoring is established.

Chapter 3 describes *cycles of inquiry*, also called *mentoring cycles*, captured in Figure 0.1. These cycles include *collaborative goal setting, classroom observations* with *data collection*, and *preparing for* and *facilitating the debrief.* These processes reflect the core of educative mentoring and set the stage for subsequently determining which practices mentors can use, and in what combination, to help teachers reach their goals.

Mentoring Practices

Chapters 4–12 detail each inside/outside practice, summarized in Table 0.1. These practices are intended to be used together, flexibly and responsively, to help teachers progress toward ambitious instructional goals.

Chapters 4–9 focus specifically on *outside* practices that occur before or after the teacher's instruction, including debriefing sessions, brief interactions, co-planning and resource support, video analysis, collegial visits, and demonstrations and rehearsals. We begin with outside practices as they tend to occur with more frequency and are good starting points for mentors to build and deepen their practice.

Chapters 10–12 describe *inside* practices, which include stepping in, demonstration teaching, and co-teaching. These tend to occur with less frequency, yet can be particularly effective when used with skill and intentionality (Gardiner & Weisling, 2016).

Even though inside and outside practices are complementary, we discuss each separately in Chapters 4–12 in order to delve deeply into each practice.

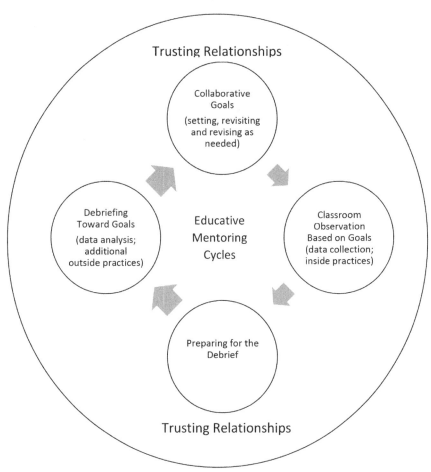

Figure 0.1. Educative mentoring cycle

Our aim is to help mentors

- have a shared language for mentoring—between mentors and between teachers and mentors—to increase collaboration and responsiveness;
- deeply understand each practice and support increasingly skilled implementation;
- address strengths, challenges, and strategies for mitigating challenges unique to each practice; and
- broaden mentors' repertoire and help mentors use the practices in thoughtful combination, so they can mentor with even more range and impact.

When mentors understand the purpose, benefits, and considerations of each practice, they are better able to select among the practices, use them in

Table 0.1.   Inside and outside mentoring practices

Inside practices: Students are present and the mentor is taking an active role in supporting instruction at that moment	*Outside* practices: Before and after instruction and/or when the teacher's students are not present
• Stepping in • Demonstration teaching • Co-teaching	• Debriefing sessions • Brief interactions • Co-planning and resource support • Video analysis • Collegial visits (occur during instruction in another teacher's classroom) • Demonstrations and rehearsals

flexible combination, and mentor responsively. To help mentors accomplish this, each chapter includes

- a description of the mentoring practice, including benefits, caveats and considerations, and rationale for its use;
- recommendations for principled implementation of each mentoring practice;
- ideas for how to incorporate the focal practice with other inside and outside practices;
- considerations for when, if, how, why, and why not to implement this practice; and
- discussion questions to facilitate reflection and action.

The goal of these combined chapters is to provide mentors with a varied repertoire of practices that they feel confident in using to support teachers' professional development and promote ambitious instruction for all students. Yet, we also recognize that to do this, mentors need opportunities for targeted and intentional development and support as well. Therefore, Chapters 13–16 shift the focus to fostering mentor growth.

Mentoring the Mentor

We believe that investing in mentor development, across a mentor's career, is also an investment in teachers and students. Therefore, Chapters 13–16 explore the processes and structures that mentors have found particularly effective in supporting *their* ongoing professional learning (Gardiner & Weisling, 2016, 2018).

FINAL THOUGHTS ON THE STRUCTURE OF THIS BOOK

Taken collectively or in individual chapter explorations, we hope to provide mentors and mentoring programs with a useful, relevant, and supportive text that helps reinforce the practices they are already using, while encouraging all mentors to expand their repertoires. All of this is done in the sake of putting a highly efficacious, well-supported educator in front of every single student.

Part I

Foundations of Effective Mentoring

Chapter One

Educative Mentoring

A Fundamental Shift in Mentoring

In our initial trainings we learned to support reflection, but that's really just a small piece of the mentoring experience. I'm learning that I just don't have enough tools to support my teachers.—Tom, first grade teacher mentoring preservice teachers

As a mentor, I'm not making decisions but guiding my teachers to make their own decisions on how to most effectively teach their students.—Greta, first-year mentor

Educative mentoring is intended to facilitate growth and provide support for all teachers across their career spans. In order to understand what educative mentoring is, why it is valuable, and how it can be enacted, it is important to first understand some of the history of mentoring. This background helps explain some of the ambiguities surrounding mentoring and why having a vision of mentoring (i.e., educative mentoring) and the ability to act upon that vision with purpose is imperative.

MENTORING: A BRIEF HISTORY

For the better part of the last 20 or so years, mentoring was aimed at *new teacher retention*. And for good reason! Upward of 40% of new teachers leave the profession within their first five years (Gurarino, Santibañez, & Daley, 2006; Ingersoll, Merrill, Stuckey, & Collins, 2018). These numbers are even higher when teachers work in poverty-impacted communities and with students of color (Simon & Moore-Johnson, 2015).

Further compounding this problem is the fact that it takes potentially five years for teachers to develop high levels of expertise (Berliner, 2001). The revolving door of teachers means that too many students never get teachers capable of the kind of ambitious instruction that can make a difference in their life opportunities. It also demonstrates a system and a profession that does not adequately take care of its newest members, tragically wasting human potential.

For these reasons and more, finding ways to support the retention of new teachers is an important goal. It is no surprise that many of the early, as well as some of the current, aims of mentoring programs were to keep teachers teaching. The most common ways of doing this were to identify skillful teachers who were also emphatic and experienced in the school or school system and transition them into the role of mentor. They were typically called upon to provide emotional support through rough patches and to help teachers fit into their new school and school district. Evidence suggests that these efforts did reduce teacher attrition (Ingersoll & Strong, 2011).

However, while retention-oriented mentoring can keep teachers in the field, it does not guarantee they will become more knowledgeable and skilled professionals (Wang & Odell, 2002). In order to meet more rigorous content standards and to ensure all students receive ambitious and equitable instruction, teachers need supports that span their careers and focus on both emotional support and long-term professional growth (Feiman-Nemser, 2012).

MENTORING IN THE CURRENT CONTEXT: EDUCATIVE MENTORING

Based on the understanding that retention is important but insufficient, mentoring programs have reoriented toward helping teachers enact ambitious instruction, improve student learning, and see successes more quickly. To do this, mentors need to have a clear vision for the aims of their work. That vision becomes the North Star that helps them navigate all the complexities they encounter as they mentor.

A vision does not tell mentors *how* to mentor, but it does provide a framework for making decisions and reflecting upon those decisions. *Educative mentoring* fits squarely in this expanded view of mentoring and has the potential to both increase teacher retention *and* more quickly help teachers across career phases develop expertise. Educative mentoring is the following:

- *Collaborative*: Mentors and teachers work together as equals.
- *Situated*: Mentoring occurs in-person (or virtually) in the teacher's classroom to ensure support is contextualized and personalized.

- *Goal driven*: Mentors and teachers set specific, individualized, and ambitious instructional goals to guide each phase of their work together.
- *Scaffolded*: Mentors help deconstruct teachers' goals into sequential, actionable steps and draw upon a range of mentoring practices to support teacher learning toward that goal.
- *Equity oriented*: Because the goals of teaching are to ensure *everyone* has access to rigorous learning opportunities, equity is inextricably linked to teacher's goals. Mentors and teachers must work with intentionality to ensure that, whatever they are working on, it is for the good of all students, with special attention to students who have traditionally been marginalized.
- *Individualized and responsive*: Mentoring is not a sequence of "one size fits all" steps. Mentors take their lead from teachers' goals, strengths and needs, learning preferences, and other information as they create and adjust teacher-centered plans that balance movement toward goals and flexibility in how that process unfolds.
- *Ongoing*: To make a difference in teacher learning, mentoring must happen regularly. A commitment to mentoring would include, at minimum, 1 to 2 years of weekly mentoring cycles. These cycles would include classroom observations and debriefing sessions scheduled on the same day, or at least within 24–48 hours of each other. In contexts where this is simply not possible, mentors and teachers would do the best they can to meet regularly and in predictable ways, and consider the potential offered by technology.

INSIDE/OUTSIDE FRAMEWORK OF MENTORING PRACTICES

Taken together, the aims and processes described above create a vision for each mentor's practice. Yet, vision alone does not help mentors effectively support teacher learning. To link the vision of educative mentoring with concrete strategies, Schwille (2008) drew upon observations and interviews of mentors who enact an educative practice. She identified a set of practices these mentors used and grouped them into two categories of practice: those that happen *inside* the action of teaching and those that happen *outside* the action of teaching.

Inside practices include mentors' active engagement with the teachers' students *during* instruction. Inside practices include co-teaching, stepping in, and demonstration teaching. Using inside practices stems from the belief that "real time" support with the teacher's own students contextualizes the focal goal in ways that better and more quickly scaffold teachers' learning.

Outside practices include debriefing sessions, brief interactions, co-planning and procuring resources, video analysis, co-observing in another classroom (i.e., collegial visits), and demonstrations and rehearsals, practices that all occur when *the teacher's students are not present*. Using outside practices stems from the belief that the deep processing, problem solving, and reflection that occurs with a skilled, responsive mentor provides the time and space to help teachers learn in and from their practice.

Inside and outside practices are complementary, designed to be used together with purpose and flexibility. These practices occur within and throughout mentoring cycles and will be discussed in depth in Chapters 4–12. Mentors and teachers collaborate to make decisions about which practices to use, when, how, and in what combination. These practices are always in the service of teachers' learning and helping teachers achieve their goals for ambitious instruction.

A MYTH ABOUT MENTORS

If mentors are to effectively meet the aims of educative mentoring, they must have a very specific skill set. There is an all-too-common myth that "good teachers make good mentors." Anyone who has transitioned from the classroom into supervising preservice or mentoring in-service teachers will find that they do in fact tap into a skill set that connects to effective teaching. This includes rapport building, analyzing student work, and pulling from a robust set of instructional activities (IA). They will also be quick to tell you that in many other places, the required skill set diverges.

Unfortunately, too many mentors have been left to draw upon their former skill set alone to mentor: their interpersonal strengths, their knowledge of schools and school systems, and their own expertise as teachers. These skills are definite assets. Mentors should absolutely demonstrate empathy and be good listeners; teachers need to be heard and have a chance to process their experiences. However, these are not comprehensive enough to intentionally support the knowledge and skills teachers need to enact ambitious instruction for all students.

Certainly, being an effective teacher is another important skill set for mentors to have, but it is also insufficient. In an ever-evolving field like education, mentors will ultimately find themselves mentoring in content areas and grade levels they never experienced. Mentors may find themselves helping teachers navigate IAs, standards, and curricula they never taught. They will work with adults, fostering learning *about teaching* and supporting the acquisition of IAs more so than implementing them. They will also find themselves in a different level of leadership within the school/system.

To truly help teachers become more knowledge, equitable, and impactful, mentors must not only draw on skills they developed in the classroom but also develop a clear vision of mentoring as well as a knowledge base and apply skills that includes

- cultivating dispositions on reflection that include open-mindedness and intellectual responsibility;
- helping teachers recognize, identify, and prioritize problems of practice;
- facilitating analysis, problem posing, and problem solving;
- helping teachers design responsive, ambitious teaching and learning experiences that also include analyzing, using, and adapting available curricular resources; creating and sustaining an equitable learning community; drawing upon students' intellectual, social, and cultural resources; and collaborating with families;
- fostering relationships with teachers, students, and administrators (see Chapter 2);
- noting, naming, and discussing strengths and areas of growth;
- reinforcing an understanding of theory and how it links to effective practice;
- modeling curiosity and dispositions of and skills to facilitate continuous growth;
- setting clear goals related to ambitious instruction and enacting a *mentoring cycle* (see Chapter 3) to help teachers attain their goals;
- selecting and implementing a wide range of inside *and* outside practices to scaffold teacher learning (see Chapters 4–12); and
- helping teachers learn in and from their teaching.

In no way are these examples meant to be a definitive list (let alone a checklist)! Rather, it is a starting point for mentoring programs and mentors who strive to maximize the impact of their work with teachers and students.

FINAL THOUGHTS ON EDUCATIVE MENTORING

Mentoring teachers across their careers is a practice ripe with potential. An effective mentor can support new teachers' transitions into the workplace and accelerate teachers' learning across their career, which in turn can support students' learning. Educative mentoring is complex work. For mentors to meet its full potential, they need comprehensive professional learning and support in order to have a serious and sustained impact on teacher and student learning.

QUESTIONS FOR REFLECTION AND ACTION

1. In what ways, as a mentor or mentee, have you experienced educative mentoring? What aspects were in place? Were there gaps? In what ways, if any, do you draw upon your experiences being mentored to mentor teachers?
2. Does the educative framework inform how you currently mentor teachers? What might be the opportunities for and challenges of mentoring from an educative framework?
3. What questions are you left with after reading this chapter? What are you most interested in reading and learning throughout this book?

Chapter Two

Trust

The Cornerstone for Educative Mentoring

It took me a while to trust my mentor. To realize she was there to support and not judge. Once I did, I opened up. I wasn't afraid to ask questions and then things really changed.—Keisha, a first-year teacher

Trust is the foundation of all mentoring. How can anyone learn if they don't trust you?—April, a fifth-year instructional coach

Educative mentoring, by its very nature, requires that teachers engage in introspection and be willing to act on critical feedback. That is hard work and requires high levels of trust between teachers and mentors. It is difficult to imagine teachers setting authentic goals, opening up their classrooms, and sharing their vulnerabilities if trust is not present. At the same time, it is difficult to imagine mentors having truly authentic conversations or implementing a full range of mentoring practices without *mutual trust* with their teachers. For both mentors and teachers to embrace mentoring, and apply the full range of inside and outside mentoring practices, they need to see each other as reliable, trustworthy, and capable.

While essential, mutual trust between mentor and teacher is not enough to ensure teachers' learning is maximized. To fully realize the aims of educative mentoring, mentors must also establish and maintain strong relationships with their teachers' students and administrators. Trust across all invested stakeholders, while a significant investment, is critical to successful educative mentoring.

BUILDING TRUST WITH TEACHERS

As trust between mentors and their teachers is built, buy-in for mentoring and for the risk-taking that educative mentoring requires increases. When trust is present, teachers are more likely to ask even their most vulnerable questions, acknowledge gaps in their practice, reflect openly, work through tensions that may arise, and schedule observations at the times when they most need their mentor's support.

Teachers will also be more willing to work through difficult conversations about teaching and learning such as if mentors' observations indicate patterns of inequity or low expectations. Likewise, mentors are more likely to put themselves into the more vulnerable positions required of inside practices like demonstration (see Chapter 11) and co-teaching (see Chapter 12) when their relationships with their teachers are firmly rooted in trust.

When trust is not yet present or relationships are in early stages, some teachers may feel reluctant to fully invest in mentoring. They may fear looking incompetent in front of their mentor or students. They may be unduly hard on themselves and think that their mentor will reinforce their own negative perceptions. They may believe their mentor will be judgmental. In short, when trust is not developed, many teachers will put up guards that interfere with learning.

One way mentors can build strong, foundational relationships at the beginning of the school year is by helping teachers set up their classrooms, reviewing initial lesson plans, and offering "quick wins," feedback that is brief, is relatively easy to implement, and should produce immediate and positive results. While the core of educative mentoring revolves around the in-depth learning that comes from mentoring cycles, these interactions help each teacher start the year off right and with confidence in their mentor. Supporting teachers in this way can also build mentor credibility in the eyes of their teachers, which is another critical component of trusting teacher-mentor relationships.

Much has already been written about why trust between teachers and mentors is important as well as ways to establish trust (cf. Aguilar, 2013; Bloom, Castagna, Moir, & Warren, 2005). Among the most important ideas is that building trust takes time and requires effort and intentionality. Mentors build and sustain trust over time by

- being professionally *and* emotionally supportive (focusing on professional knowledge, while also recognizing the importance of holistic support);
- being collaborative and showing mentors are *partners* in teachers' development;
- refraining from judgment;

- being adaptive and flexible in order to be responsive to teachers' evolving needs and concerns;
- investing time throughout the year to get to know teachers' professional goals and aspirations; educational beliefs and philosophies; personal interests, experiences, and life outside of work; and communication styles, and how and when teachers like to process experiences and receive feedback (e.g., time of day, phone-text-email, direct or reflective);
- following through on supports and actions promised;
- maintaining confidentiality;
- being honest about their own (mentor's) knowledge and experiences; and
- being a consistent, supportive, honest presence.

With strong mentor-teacher relationships in place, both parties are willing to be more open and engage meaningfully in the work required of educative mentoring.

BUILDING TRUST WITH STUDENTS

While it is well established that mentors must build trust with the teachers they are supporting, it is less well known that strong mentor-student relationships are also important. Learning students' names is a good start. Mentors should also learn students' interests, strengths, and needs. This specific knowledge becomes a foundation for providing even more contextualized and responsive feedback and support to teachers.

Additionally, when mentors build relationships with students, they can draw upon a wider repertoire of mentoring practices. Specifically, when mentors know students and are seen as part of the classroom community, mentoring practices like demonstration and co-teaching (see Chapters 11 and 12), video analysis (see Chapter 7) , and stepping in (see Chapter 10) are far more likely to unfold in ways that reflect classroom needs, to build upon teachers' and students' strengths, and to contribute to learning. Otherwise, these practices can be disruptive and fail to fulfill their potential.

Many teachers welcome mentors' active presence with students. Yet others may have an image of an "unobtrusive" mentor sitting in the back of the classroom. That image fails to capitalize upon the full learning potential educative mentoring offers. Therefore, mentors should help teachers understand why it is important for *mentors* to also build relationships with students and interact with students when they are in the classroom. With the rationale of supporting everyone's learning in mind, mentors and teachers can identify ways to purposefully integrate mentors into the classroom life.

BUILDING TRUST WITH ADMINISTRATORS

Among their many responsibilities, school administrators (e.g., principals, assistant principals) have the role of determining building initiatives and ensuring that district, state, and national policies are implemented. It is on their shoulders that the successes and shortcomings of a school ultimately fall. Therefore, they are important members of the mentoring team, and mentors will only benefit from building trusting relationships with their teachers' administrators.

Like any important activity, building and sustaining the mentor-administrator relationship is nuanced. First, some mentors, especially those early in their careers who may have just transitioned from a role wherein the administrator was their direct boss, may feel discomfort in the new dynamic. This can translate to uncertainty about *how* and *when* to communicate about their teachers to the administrator.

Mentors can address this potential concern by dedicating time early in their mentoring to sit with the administrator in order to get to know one another, to learn about the administrator's goals and priorities for the year, and to understand their thoughts about mentoring. At this same time, mentors can explain their mentoring priorities and expectations (programmatic and/or personal), if they are not already known to the administrator. Chief among these initial conversations is establishing a shared priority—students.

Second, and related to the first concern, trusting relationships among and between mentor, teacher, and administrator are paramount to educative mentoring. Because of their unique role, mentors can sometimes find themselves in a confusing position of determining what information can and should be shared with which party, while still maintaining the appropriate trust and confidence. A teacher may worry and wonder about how information from their mentoring is being shared with their administrators, or what information administrators share with mentors. Mentors can prevent some of these concerns by establishing clear protocols of communication, and being transparent with each party about what information is being shared.

Finally, administrators have the role of determining building initiatives as well as following state, federal, and district mandates. Depending on their context, mentors can sometimes find themselves "stuck in the middle" of differing and even competing priorities that may complicate setting authentic goals with teachers. Once again, establishing clear lines of regular communication and trust-based relationships can mitigate these concerns.

When competing priorities do emerge, mentors can draw upon their knowledge of administrators', the teacher's, and students' needs to

- make the building priority the sole focus of subsequent mentoring, while making clear that the teacher's goal is important and projecting when they might focus on that goal;
- work with administrators to scaffold the teacher's present performance toward the given priority;
- merge the teacher's, mentor's, and administrator's priorities; or
- advocate for a different priority, explaining why a different focus will lead to better long-term outcomes.

Sometimes relationship development with administrators is seamless, and other times it may require more thoughtful effort, especially if there are differing priorities. However, educative mentors who purposefully build relationships with administrators are in a better position to be an effective negotiator, ally, and partner.

PROACTIVELY ADDRESSING POTENTIAL CONCERNS

Trust—among teachers, mentors, students, and administrators—is the foundation for productive mentoring relationships. It also cannot be taken for granted. As mentioned here and in ample other mentoring resources, it takes significant time and effort to cultivate and sustain trust (Aguilar, 2013; Bloom et al., 2005). Mentors and/or mentoring programs must delegate time and resources to this process, rather than expect teachers and mentors to jump directly into the complex work of improving teaching and learning. Even in the most urgent contexts, where high-quality teaching is most needed, investing time and energy into relationship building is a worthwhile endeavor.

Trust is also something that sometimes has to be repaired. It is inevitable that nerves will fray, particularly when teachers, or mentors, feel overwhelmed, or miscommunications occur. For example, a mentor's feedback may inadvertently offend a teacher during a debriefing session (see Chapter 4). Or, when a mentor offers to demonstrate or co-teach (see Chapters 11 and 12), the teacher takes it as a sign the mentor thinks they are incompetent. In other cases, teachers may fail to follow through on mentoring next steps that were set during debriefing sessions, which mentors could misinterpret as resistance. Also, at some point, mentors may need to deliver feedback, particularly around equity, that is hard for the teacher to hear.

In any of these very real examples, among myriad others, relationships may falter or even break down. In order for the partnership to successfully move forward, mentors will have to invest in "clearing the air" and rebuilding their relationship.

FINAL THOUGHTS ABOUT TRUST

Educative mentoring is premised on the belief that, with collaborative, responsive, and scaffolded support, teachers can see dramatic improvements in their teaching. To achieve this end, mentors must use a wide range of mentoring practices, the success of which hinge on *trusting relationships* between and across invested stakeholders. Mentoring programs must therefore dedicate time and energy to establishing and sustaining thoughtful, responsive, and purposeful relationships across and between mentors and teachers, students, and administrators.

QUESTIONS FOR REFLECTION AND ACTION

1. Think about the teachers, mentors, and others from whom you have learned the most: How did they establish trust so that learning could happen?
2. Review the list of suggestions to build and sustain trust. Which do you already do? What else might you add? What can you do to expand the ways you foster trusting relationships?
3. What ideas and recommendations do you have for building trust with students and administrators? What steps might you take to advance trust with students? With administrators?

Chapter Three

Goal Setting and Collecting Useful Data Within the Mentoring Cycle

Collecting and using data intentionally means the information I'm giving the teachers is based on something factual rather than just me trying to make a suggestion based on my opinion alone. The data is almost like another set of eyes for the teacher too. When you're in front of a whole class of students, you don't necessarily always see what each student's doing and understanding. Data can help the teacher better understand their own practice, see patterns and areas of strength and growth.—Joelle, a first-year mentor

How do mentors know where or how to start their work with teachers? What should they focus on? How can they make the most positive impact on a teacher's practice? How do they help the teachers they are mentoring "see," learn from, and continue to improve their classroom instruction? These important questions get at the core of mentoring.

It all begins with the *mentoring cycle*. The mentoring cycle, represented in Figure 3.1, consists of goal setting, classroom observations where data related to that goal are collected, and planning for and facilitating debriefing sessions. Through this process, teachers and mentors reflect on progress toward goals and continue the cycle. This chapter focuses on setting goals and collecting goal-aligned data to be used in the debrief.

COLLABORATIVE GOAL SETTING

Mentoring cycles formally begin with *collaborative goal setting* where mentors and teachers meet to discuss and prioritize the goals for ambitious instruction that will guide their work. Goals should be driven by the teacher's priorities but will also be informed by data that mentors collect during class-

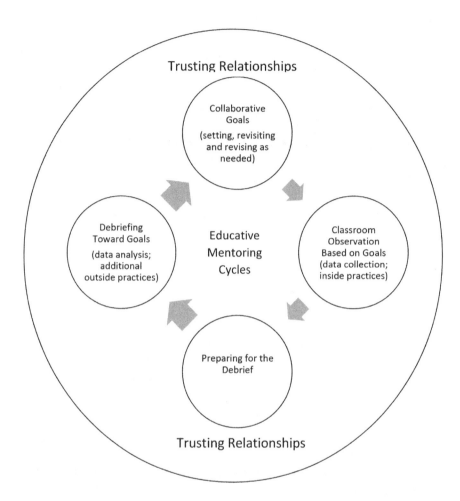

Figure 3.1. Educative mentoring cycle

room observations, school and district initiatives, and feedback from building administrators. As educative mentoring is teacher centered, the best goals are the ones that matter to the teacher and that will lead to more equitable and ambitious teaching.

Once established, that goal guides all subsequent mentoring work. From the types of data that will be collected to how debriefing sessions are framed and to which inside/outside practices are employed, the goal is always front and center. Of course, topics beyond the goal will enter into discussions, but full efforts should be directed toward keeping the focus on the goal while responding to teachers in ethical and responsive ways. Otherwise, efforts can be diluted.

IDEAS FOR GOAL SETTING

Early on in a teacher's career, mentors may need to provide more goal-setting guidance, with the idea that, over time, teachers will take on more ownership for setting their own goals. New teachers' goals can sometimes be vague, broad, and overwhelming. They may need help prioritizing and making sure goals are specific and actionable. Experienced teachers are more likely to have effective habits of goal setting but can still benefit from collaborative problem solving and knowledgeable colleagues' perspectives.

At the beginning of the year, goals will often relate to establishing a positive and productive classroom environment, especially for early career teachers. That said, mentors should still encourage a focus on instruction. After all, a productive classroom environment is inextricably linked with relevant, supported, and rigorous learning.

The following is a starting set of potential goals teachers and mentors can consider and build from throughout the school year:

- Organizing and maximizing the use of physical space, seating, materials, and so forth, and ensuring the space is inclusive and diversity responsive
- Designing logical, developmentally appropriate, and time-saving routines and procedures, as well as *how* to implement them
- Increasing students' active engagement in rigorous instructional activities (IA)
- Shifting from teacher-centered to student-centered instruction
- Expanding teachers' repertoires by including new IAs
- Refining teachers' use of existing IAs to promote equity, inclusion, and achievement
- Fostering a collaborative classroom community
- Providing instructional scaffolding that gradually shifts responsibility to students
- Planning multiday sequences of lessons, as opposed to day-by-day planning
- Motivating students to take instructional risks and to invest in their own, and each other's, learning
- Locating and using school and district resources, noting where they need to be adapted to represent *and* be responsive to all learners
- Implementing culturally responsive and sustaining teaching that, along with other concepts already described (see Gay, 2018; Ladson-Billings, 2014; Paris, 2012), promotes students' voices and is empowering; centers learning around multiple perspectives, especially those that have been historically marginalized; is rigorous and student and community driven; honors and integrates students' funds of knowledge (Moll, Amati, Neff, &

Gomez, 1992); and helps students see how they can use their knowledge to act purposefully in the world

- Communicating effectively with families and other service providers (e.g., social workers, speech/language pathologists, co-teachers)
- Responding to student behavior effectively and in a way that is minimally disruptive and fully respectful to all learners
- Gathering and using data from a range of sources to inform instruction

While these goals are broad and not intended to be an exhaustive list, they are a starting point to promote thinking and reflection. If mentors and teachers choose to draw from these goals, they should be contextualized (i.e., adjusted for the teacher's specific circumstances), and possibly sequenced into sub-goals, to meet teachers and their students' needs.

COLLECTING FOCUSED DATA

Once goals are set, teachers need ways to assess their progress. They need to see and understand what is working well and why, how to build upon their successes, and when and how to adjust. Data collection gives teachers the information they need for reflection and continuous learning.

For data to be useful, data collection needs to be centered on an observational focus. For example, say a teacher set a goal of initiating student-led book discussions. There are many facets that go into productive discussions, which means there are many potential observational foci. The mentor and teacher should pick one that they believe will be most useful *at this time, based on the teacher's current performance* to help them meet this goal.

For example, informed by prior data analysis, the teacher and mentor believe students need more language support to engage in meaningful student-led literature discussions. The pair determine that prior to the next observation, the teacher will co-create an anchor chart with their students that provides a range of language stems students can draw upon during discussion. Then, the mentor will observe during literature discussions and collect data on student talk. That focused data will help the teacher analyze progress toward their goal and respond accordingly.

When the mentor collects data, for them to best facilitate teacher learning, they need to be objective. Yes, anything observed is filtered through prior experience, yet the goal is to capture observable language or behaviors, *not* insert opinions. Data also need to be presented in clear, organized ways so that teachers can co-construct knowledge from the data.

Based on the example above, a mentor stating "I think the anchor chart is working" is not particularly helpful. Rather, to fully help the teacher see the impact of incorporating the anchor chart, the mentor should script out (see

"Selective Scripting" below) the language students used during the discussion along with noting who used the chart, how, and with what frequency. The next section provides tools for data collection that can capture focused, objective data.

DATA COLLECTION TOOLS AND TIPS

Mentors have a range of data collection tools at their disposal. Some of the more versatile tools include selective scripting, seating charts/classroom mapping, checklists, and video recording. While not a comprehensive list, these tools can be used to

- capture teacher and student talk,
- show patterns of movement or usage of classroom space,
- reveal how students respond to the teacher's instruction,
- record precise elements of instructional delivery,
- show how students engage with each other and the content, and
- reveal patterns of inequity.

Based on previous discussions with the teacher, when mentors enter the classroom they know what their observational focus is. They may have also decided upon which tool to use. Or they may take a few minutes to determine which is the best way to support teacher learning in that moment. Regardless, each tool presents a way to help teachers gain a fuller perspective of teaching and learning.

Selective Scripting

Selective scripting helps teachers understand language in the classroom—clarity, rigor, use of academic language and relevant examples, patterns of talk, and much more. When using selective scripting, mentors write or type, verbatim, a preidentified subset (i.e., selective) of classroom talk. That scripting can include capturing the language spoken by the teacher and/or students during a lesson or portion of a lesson. Scripting can be based on whole-class, small-group, or even one-on-one interactions. Mentors can also time stamp their scripting, which can reveal additional pertinent information, such as the length of instructional teacher talk and/or time between opportunities for students to meaningfully engage with content.

The key to effective selective scripting includes being specific and manageable about what is scripted and using a system (shorthand, typed, recorded then typed, etc.) that allows for maximum detail and accuracy related to the focus. Multiple tools can be used to selectively script, but the most popular consists of one, two, or three columns to record teacher language/

actions, student language/actions, and/or mentor reflections (see example in Appendix A).

Seating Charts/Classroom Mapping

Seating charts/classroom mapping can be used to collect a wide range of classroom data. This process typically begins with the mentor creating by hand or with an electronic tool a visual representation of the space being observed. This could be a "map" of the whole class, a specific small group, or an individual student's seat. Once a representation is created, data can be collected to show teacher and/or student movement, student engagement, use of resources and materials, and more. Mentors typically develop their own systems of coding/shorthand to allow them to effectively collect meaningful data that can then be analyzed alongside their teacher in the debrief (see examples and support resources in Appendix A).

Checklists

Checklists typically take an IA, such as a writing mini-lesson, and break it down into its component parts. Mentors may find task analysis helpful in deconstructing an IA (see example in Appendix A). During the observation, the mentor then looks for specific evidence of each element of the IA via selective scripting, coding, student work samples, or other data points.

Analysis of the data for each element can help the teacher and mentor identify where the teacher is successfully implementing the IA, where changes are warranted, and where additional mentoring support is needed. Relatedly, the act of deconstructing steps alone may also help a teacher better understand and implement the IA.

Video Recording

Using video to record a teacher's instruction is a powerful tool for facilitating growth. Take, for example, a subgoal of enacting writing mini-lessons—one part of a teacher's larger goal of improving their writing workshop. The mentor and teacher may choose to have the mentor video the teacher implementing the writing workshop, including the mini-lesson, to capture all facets of teaching and learning. There are other important ways to capture and use video to support teacher and mentor growth. Respectively, these will be discussed in depth in Chapters 7 and 14.

BEING TRUSTWORTHY AND ADAPTIVE

Regardless of the data collection method, educative mentoring is built on trust between mentors and teachers (see Chapter 2). As such, mentors should approach observations and data collection with integrity toward and in alignment with a predetermined goal. And yet, there are times when mentors will need to make in-the-moment adjustments as appropriate. These adjustments tend to follow three primary paths.

First, mentors may need to *slightly shift the type of data collected for the shared focus*. For example, a mentor may have intended to selectively script all questions asked by the teacher. During the debrief, their plan is to sort questions by level of rigor. However, while collecting these data, the mentor begins to notice some concerning patterns related to, but going beyond, rigor. The mentor may decide to reconfigure their scripting to identify who is being asked which types of questions, who is volunteering, and/or who is being called upon. In this way, integrity toward the shared goal is maintained while inequities in instruction are revealed that must be critically examined.

Next, sometimes a mentor will observe a teacher incorrectly teaching content. No matter the intended method or topic of data collection, when teachers deliver inaccurate instruction or seem to be at a loss for how to convey ideas or respond to students, mentors should feel empowered to pause their data collection and *step in to clarify or model a portion of the lesson*. Students deserve accurate content.

Finally, on occasion, mentors may need to *abandon all data collection because student safety is at risk!* Students, their learning and their safety, always takes precedence. So, if/when student safety (emotional or physical) is at immediate risk, data collection should be abandoned and the mentor should *step in to restore safety and order to the classroom*. The experience should be discussed as part of the follow-up debrief.

When it comes to stepping in to correct content or ensure student safety, mentors will need to help teachers process the experience—what happened, why, and where to go next—in the debriefing session. Strong relationships with teachers and students make stepping in less disruptive and can help minimize or mitigate any potential threats teachers feel toward their credibility and authority.

DATA CAN REVEAL INEQUITIES

Data can uncover inequitable patterns in the classroom. The largely objective nature of the data collection methods described above can also help mentors address these inequities with their teachers. Some common patterns particularly related to students of color, students from low socioeconomic status households, or students with disabilities include but are not limited to (Cazden, 2001)

- low academic expectations,
- lack of opportunity for elaborative talk to process or refine thinking, and
- teacher-centered instruction that does not foster open-ended thinking or give students the opportunities to build off of each other's thinking.

These data are important and will be discussed during the debrief. Facilitating difficult conversations where biases and inequities are addressed requires sensitivity. Mentors should have honest, data-informed conversations in order to help teachers learn, grow, and respond in ethical ways to all students. Once again, trust is critical. Teachers are more receptive to facing hard truths when not only the data are objective but also the mentor is honest, supportive, and refrains from judgment.

THE DEBRIEF

The next phase in the mentoring cycle is the debrief where data are shared and analyzed, and problem solving occurs. Debriefing sessions help teachers make discoveries about teaching and learning, and support continued progress toward short- and long-term goals. Debriefing sessions are a critical component of the mentoring cycle and are the focus of Chapter 4.

FINAL THOUGHTS ON OBSERVING AND COLLECTING USEFUL DATA WITHIN MENTORING CYCLES

Purposeful and flexible data collection is integral to educative mentoring. Data can reveal, to mentors and teachers alike, a more comprehensive and objective view of a teacher's practice. Insights derived from data can then inform decisions for how to continuously grow as a professional and improve teaching and learning. Ultimately, data collection, like all mentoring practices, should be used responsively and deliberately to create a path by which teachers can set and meet goals related to ambitious instruction.

QUESTIONS FOR REFLECTION AND ACTION

1. Goal setting is the entry into educative mentoring and mentoring cycles. What are some specific goals you have set with teachers?
2. Review and discuss the list of potential goals. Which could you see suggesting to the teachers you work with? How might you help them unpack a broader goal so it fits their needs? What else might you add?

3. Data collection is a complex and vital part of a mentoring practice. It helps teachers "see" their classroom in new and more nuanced ways. What are your experiences with collecting data?
4. Look over the tools and examples in Appendix A. Which of the data collection tools are you familiar with? What has been your experience with this/these tool(s)? What were your successes? What are your next steps for more impactful data collection?
5. Look over the tools and examples in Appendix A. Which tool would you like to try? Consider a teacher with whom you might try that tool. How would you present the tool to them? Problem-solve on how to make this tool useful in your context.

Part II

Mentoring Practices

Chapter Four

Debriefing Sessions

The Heart of Mentoring

I continue to have debriefs that are not awesome, but they're getting there. I think that early on the challenges were more like, I have all of this data, what are we really supposed to get the teacher to zone in on? How do I communicate this effectively? I'm better, but it sure is a steeper climb than I ever imagined.—Joelle, first-year mentor

In a debrief there is a very dire sense of urgency for students. You want teachers to see what you are seeing and make changes. At the same time, you want that teacher to compose their own ideas and come to their own conclusions; that's when mentoring is most powerful, when teachers own the change and learn the habits of mind to sustain and continue to grow. What you as a mentor need to do and say are the right things to help the teacher get to that thing that they need to think about and reflect on.—Kelsey, fifth-year mentor

The debrief is truly the heart of mentoring. It is a dedicated time and space for mentors and teachers to come together for the kind of deep analysis and problem solving that leads to meaningful instructional change. In a *productive debrief* mentors share data collected during the prior observation, actively engage teachers in their own learning, and co-create a plan to help teachers move closer toward their goals.

Fostering a productive, teacher-centered debriefing session is a deceptively complex and nuanced process. Debriefs are far more likely to foster learning and change when mentors *prepare for the debrief* and *employ a reflective protocol*. This chapter explores how and why to prepare for a debrief. Then, a framework and language stems for facilitating a debrief are offered to help new and experienced mentors alike become more intentional, responsive, and effective in supporting teacher's learning.

PLANNING THE DEBRIEFING SESSION

Skilled mentors make debriefing look easy. Yet, many novice mentors, and even some experienced ones, find that facilitating a productive debrief is highly challenging. For some, this is because they are unaware of the necessary step between data collection and debriefing: *debrief planning.*

Debrief planning is an important step that increases the likelihood that debriefs will facilitate teacher learning. Think of it this way: A teacher should not teach without intentional preparation. Similarly, a mentor should not go into a debrief without giving considerable thought to how they will help the teacher interpret collected data in ways that help them make progress toward their instructional goal.

Debrief planning begins with mentors thinking through the observation while reviewing the data collected in the classroom *and* honoring the mentoring goal. Helping teachers make useful meaning of the collected data requires significant work on the part of the mentor *before the debrief.* Specifically, mentors need time to review and reflect upon the data so that they can be a resource for learning. To do so, mentors should ask themselves questions such as follows:

- What stands out to *me* as a mentor about the teacher's present level of performance (strengths, areas of need) *related to their goal(s)*?
- Which data will be most important and impactful for the teacher to review as they relate to understanding and taking action to make progress toward their goals?
- Are data clearly presented and legible?
- Is there anything that might be confusing, challenging, disappointing, or otherwise difficult for the teacher to see and discuss?

In response to this analysis, mentors may do the following to *make data clear and meaningful for teachers*:

- Remove extraneous information *without* damaging the integrity of the data. When mentors use certain tools like selective scripting, it can be easy to capture data beyond the mentoring focus. Mentors should read through all data, and remove irrelevant data, to make sure they are accurate and reflective of mentoring goals.
- Rewrite and/or reorganize for clarity. Classroom life proceeds quickly, and mentors must capture a great deal of information as rapidly as pos-

sible to not miss anything important. At times, that leads to data that may be difficult for the teacher to read and interpret. Mentors may need to rewrite or reorganize data, paying careful attention to accuracy, so that they are clearer and easier to read and understand.

• When needed, further code the data to reveal patterns of inequities based on who is/is not engaging in learning, and in what ways/to what extent. Mentors should look across student demographics and positions in the room to see if opportunities to learn are equitable.

Once data are reviewed and made clear, concise, accurate, and goal aligned, mentors should also plan for the language they will use to foster teacher reflection of *both* instructional strengths and areas of growth. As discussed in more depth in the next section, the language stems/questions should be open-ended and designed to meaningfully engage the teacher in active reflection, analysis, and problem solving (see Aguilar, 2013; Bloom, Castagna, Moir, & Warren, 2005; Feiman-Nemser, 2012).

DEBRIEF STRUCTURE

Optimally on the same day as the observation, mentors and teachers meet for debriefing sessions that generally last between 30 and 90 minutes. At times, schedules do not align for same-day meetings. If that happens debriefs should be scheduled as soon as possible, preferably within 24–48 hours. The point is to debrief while the experience is fresh and momentum is present.

Many mentors, mentoring programs, and teacher educators are familiar with and use the framework advanced by the New Teacher Center to facilitate collaborative conversations that lead to changes in practice. In these conversations, mentors typically do the following:

• Briefly recap the goal of the observation. This may sound similar to "I came in today to collect [specific type of data] about [mentoring focus] . . ."
• Solicit teachers' analyses and reflections beginning with asking a question like "What went well [in connection to goal]?" During this time, mentors and teachers identify patterns of practice that support/facilitate student learning.
• Examine, alongside their teachers, "What challenges did you experience [in connection with the goal]?" During this time teachers reflect and analyze, interpret and co-analyze data, brainstorm ideas, and problem-solve.
• Generate *next steps for teachers and mentors*. Teachers' next steps may include what they would do to fine-tune or strengthen teaching and learning. Mentors' next steps focus on what supports teachers need from men-

tors to accomplish those next steps. This can include the full range of inside/outside mentoring practices that are discussed in upcoming chapters.

- Schedule the next time the mentor will come to the teacher's class to observe and/or implement inside practices discussed in Chapters 10–12.

This framework fits nicely within an educative orientation as it fosters teacher learning; is teacher centered, collaborative, and responsive; and is flexible in its application.

As with any framework, with time, practice, and expertise, small adjustments and innovations in use occur. The following describes some such adaptations, including language stems, that new and experienced mentors may find beneficial to include in their debrief sessions.

Reconnecting (Before Recapping the Observational Goal)

While it can be natural to want to jump into a debrief and begin the analytical and data-sharing work, it can be more effective to "go slow to go fast." That is, mentors should start by taking a few minutes to reconnect with the teacher on a personal and professional level, asking questions like "How are things going for you?" or "What is on your mind today?" and being sure to pay attention to and acknowledge what the teacher shares. This demonstrates genuine care and interest, fosters rapport, and can give a teacher a moment to vent or express concerns that may otherwise inhibit their focus.

That said, it is important that mentors do not let this portion extend and become the focus of the session. Mentors can gently turn the conversation to recapping the goal of the observation by saying something like "I have made note of these so that we can circle back to them. Are you ready to talk about [mentor goal]?"

What's Working?

The "official" debriefing sessions begin with a transition to stating the mentoring goal for the observation. The pair then spends 5 to 15 minutes discussing successes related to the goal and what contributed to those successes. Mentors want teachers to lead as much of this portion as possible.

Mentors may also need to help teachers identify "why" a certain action was effective by posing questions like "What do you think made X work/ effective?" While it is optimal if teachers name their own successes, mentors may need to provide some prompting such as "One thing I noticed was . . ." or "While you think, one thing I noticed was . . . Did/Do you notice that as well?" It can be helpful to examine the data only as they address strengths at this time.

Many teachers will want to skip over an exploration of strengths and go straight to problem solving, but this is inadvisable. First, teaching is hard and teachers should have a balanced perspective on their practice, and that includes successes. Second, if teachers name and analyze what they are doing well, they are more likely to continue doing it. Finally, pausing to recognize and "unpack" successes can help teachers identify other contexts where using this aspect of their practice might make their teaching more effective.

Should a teacher jump into challenges, mentors should validate and then redirect the conversation. For example, a mentor might say, "I'm going to make a note of that because it's very interesting/important, but for now, let's focus on/come back to what's working!" This type of prompting can actually be a handy response in multiple points in a debrief, or when debriefing a teacher who regularly takes the conversation in a multitude of directions.

It is also not uncommon for teachers, especially those who are earlier in their careers, to identify a "success" that does not reflect equitable and ambitious instruction. It may be tempting, and at times necessary, to correct their perception in that moment. However, wherever possible, it is important to maintain the celebratory nature of this portion of the debrief, making note of it and circling back: "That is something I would like us to revisit later in our conversation, so let me make a note."

What's Challenging?

Next, conversation should shift to exploring challenges. The primary goal of this 10- to 20-minute section is to help the teacher identify *what* aspects of teaching and learning (related to the goal) are not currently as effective as they could be and *why* those aspects matter. If teachers are to make meaningful change to their instruction, they need to be able to identify what needs to change and why change matters.

At this time, mentors share data and guide a problem-solving, analytical discussion. Mentors can segue into this section by either asking questions specific to the mentoring goal such as "As we talk about [instructional activity], what are you still finding challenging?" or using data to lead the teacher to the challenge, suggesting, "Take a look at the portion of our data. What do you notice about . . . ?"

Teachers, especially those new to the profession, often have a veritable laundry list of concerns and could use the entire time available in a mentoring session to list them all. You, as a mentor, may have also noticed a plethora of things that need improvement! But if the goal is to make observable and impactful change to a teacher's practice, it is important to keep the conversation focused on realistic (yet ambitious) changes related to the mentoring goal. This becomes a balancing act of listening to, validating, and helping teachers prioritize their needs.

Some tips to support mentors in this portion of the conversation include the following:

Listen for moments in the conversation that "invite" comment, sometimes called "entry points," through which you can pursue the most critical areas for growth. The following stems can be helpful:

> "I agree, let's deep dive here . . ."
> "Do you think this might be related to . . ."
> "Maybe we should explore . . ."
> "I actually think that . . . is the source . . ."
> "Your data show/I noticed . . ."
> "What do you see that . . ."

Facilitate co-analysis of data. Mentors must be careful not to ask questions they know the answer to but rather to ask questions that invite teachers' interpretation and/or help them develop and deepen habits of effective reflection. These could include the following:

> "Take a look at this section of data specifically. What does this segment of data tell you? What's important to understand about . . ."
> "When you examine these data, what do they make you think . . . why?"
> "From your recollection, what was happening during this time? What was your thinking then? Now?"
> "What might be another way of interpreting . . . ?"
> "Let's look at what the data show. Now, let's consider what they mean . . ."
> "Based on your data, what do you think if we . . ."

Commit to equitable teaching. Mentors may also need to help teachers approach and understand the data in regard to equity, specifically asking themselves, "Are there patterns where populations of students do not consistently receive equitable and ambitious instruction?" And then guiding teachers to seeing those patterns themselves. For example, "Take a look at who is and is not answering questions during this lesson. What do you notice?"

There is an abundance of ways that mentors can engage teachers in data analysis. The aim here is to provide mentors with a range of options they can intentionally pull from to help teachers accurately and comprehensively "see" teaching and learning in their classroom.

Facilitate Meaningful Change to the Teacher's Practice

Based on the data analysis and subsequent discussion, mentors and teachers should work collaboratively to actually build and/or refine the skills necessary to directly address identified challenges. This should be a very active portion of the debrief that may require mentors to use additional outside practices as needed, such as co-planning (see Chapter 6) or demonstrations and/or rehearsals (see Chapter 9).

For example, if data analysis revealed that the teacher was asking only low-rigor, "right there" questions, they may need support in developing and asking more high-rigor questions. Mentors may need to explain what makes a question low/high rigor, demonstrate how to generate such a question from the assigned material, and then work side-by-side with the teacher to generate questions for tomorrow's class.

The key here is clarity. Mentors must ensure that teachers have all that they need to be successful in their independent attempts (more on this in Chapters 6 and 9). Mentors may find it helpful to ask themselves, "What needs to happen so that both the teacher and I leave this debrief confident that the teacher can attempt to implement [x] on their own?"

Identifying Meaningful and Timely Next Steps for the Teacher and Mentor

At this point, it is time to turn to the question of what needs to happen next to ensure continued growth for this teacher. When determining next steps for the teacher, there are important considerations, including the following:

- Are there inside practices such as co-teaching, demonstration teaching, or stepping in that distribute implementation risk and increase support for the teacher's attempts?
- Are there additional resources that need to be procured?
- Might the mentor need to do some additional research or knowledge building?
- Would it be useful to connect the teacher with another teacher for a collegial visit?
- What else does the teacher need to do in order to prepare to implement the discussed change in practice?

Mentors should draw upon the full repertoire of inside/outside practices to answer these questions. More information on each of these practices can be found in Chapters 5–12.

FINAL THOUGHTS ON FACILITATING PRODUCTIVE DEBRIEFS

Debriefing is a deceptively hard, yet critically important facet of mentoring. Mentors need time for intentional planning, where data can be reviewed and questions can be designed, so that the impact of the debrief on teacher practice can be maximized. Mentors also need to recognize the complexity of a debriefing session. While challenging, debriefing sessions can be highly rewarding. It is where mentors can witness and foster learning—learning that can have a positive and lasting impact on teachers and students.

QUESTIONS FOR REFLECTION AND ACTION

1. What has your experience been in planning for debriefing sessions? What from this chapter might you try? What other recommendations would you offer?
2. Drawing from the framework and language stems presented in this chapter, what are you presently using/doing? How has that affected teacher learning and development?
3. Drawing from the framework and language stems presented in this chapter, what could you add to deepen your mentoring practice? How would you see this addition affecting teacher learning and development?
4. The debriefing session is where critical analyses and sometimes hard conversations occur. Have you had experience with this type of debrief? If so, how do you feel the conversation went? Why? Were there ideas from this chapter that may have been helpful to this conversation?
5. Collaboration and mutual responsibility are important concepts in educative mentoring. What can you do to get teachers, over time, to take on more leadership in the debrief?

Chapter Five

Brief Interactions

Making the Most of a Few Minutes

> Brief interactions with teachers build trust and show I'm there for them. They
> see that they can reach out to me for anything.—Kelsey, fifth-year mentor

Teachers and mentors wear multiple hats as they strive to ensure that all learners receive ambitious, responsive instruction. It can be difficult for both teachers and mentors to keep up with all of their professional responsibilities, let alone maintain meaningful connections with one another. This can be especially true for mentors who also have their own classrooms (i.e., are not full release), for mentors who work with teachers or student teachers across multiple buildings, or mentors who have a large caseload of teachers to support.

Connections are also difficult to sustain when there are frequent interruptions to mentoring, such as during testing windows or holiday breaks. In short, in the busyness of school life, mentors may find it challenging to sustain the levels of trust and contextual knowledge needed to mentor responsively. Brief interactions and drop-ins (a type of brief interaction) are mentoring practices that can be used to respond to these challenges.

BRIEF INTERACTIONS

Brief interactions are quick, informal, often unscheduled encounters between mentors and teachers that build and sustain relationships, provide quick and impromptu support, and maintain momentum throughout the mentoring cycle. Brief interactions can be in person, such as touching base briefly or passing along a note and/or materials in the hall, or virtual, including email-ing, texting, and video conferencing. Through brief interactions mentors can

- get a sense of how the teacher is doing or feeling;
- quickly follow up on a question or concern;
- provide a resource promised in a debriefing session;
- check in on a student or situation of concern without waiting for the next scheduled meeting;
- engage in quick problem solving with the teacher;
- gain insights into how progress toward the instructional goal is going; and
- show the teacher the mentor is thinking about them, invested in their success, and willing to help out as needed.

On occasion, mentors may also opt to use a brief interaction as an opportu-nity to take on a temporary assistive role. For example, if a specials class (e.g., art, PE) or outdoor recess was canceled and the teacher needs a quick break or moment to gather instructional materials, a mentor may briefly watch the class. Or perhaps another teacher is absent and now another 15 students have entered the room because no substitutes were available. In that case, a mentor may help the teacher gather the additional materials needed. These actions show the mentor's commitment to building and sustaining relationships and investing in the teacher's success.

However, there is a delicate balance to this. On one hand, such actions build trust and demonstrate a mentor's commitment. On the other hand, mentors need to be careful that the focus of mentoring or expectations for mentors do not shift from fostering instructional development to providing short-term relief.

As mentors regularly and responsively engage in brief interactions, trust is enhanced and mentors develop a more comprehensive image of teachers' classrooms. This in turn can solidify the foundation of their working relation-ship for when mentors need to initiate harder conversations related to equity, rapport, and instruction. While never easy, these conversations tend to go better when teachers know their mentor is highly invested in them. Brief interactions reinforce that investment.

As maintaining continuity of support is a core aspect of this practice, brief interactions are most effective when they, on average, occur weekly. Re-member, these interactions can include emails, text messages, and passed notes, each of which takes just a few minutes of effort for rather impressive relational payoff. However, if brief interactions start to feel like an item on a "to do" list, they are no longer serving the intended purpose and should not be forced. The point is to sustain continuity and strengthen relationships in a flexible and responsive manner.

There are particular times when it is worth the time investment to have more frequent brief interactions:

- In the beginning of the year when relationships are being initially established
- When a teacher is working through a challenging experience (professional or personal) or learning goal
- Before and/or after using a new mentoring practice, particularly co-teaching or demonstration teaching (see Chapters 11 and 12) or video analysis (see Chapter 7). This provides teachers with the opportunity to share their comfort (or lack therefore) with a given mentoring practice
- When testing, field trips, assemblies, illness, or other factors such as cancelled recess or specials interrupt regularly scheduled mentoring

Mentors should get to know and be responsive to teachers' preferences for when and how brief interactions occur. Some teachers may appreciate seeing their mentors at the end of the day or during a preparatory period, while some might not. Some teachers appreciate texts, while others prefer emails. When mentors consistently incorporate teachers' preferences, they maximize the positive relational impacts of brief interactions.

DROP-INS

Drop-ins are a more structured type of brief interactions and are unscheduled observations lasting no more than 10 minutes that include quick, specific, written feedback. At the end of the observation, the mentor leaves a note that names and describes one or two effective aspects (e.g., instructional activities, ways of engaging students) observed in the classroom *and* one or two "quick wins" (i.e., suggestions) that could be implemented easily and immediately, and positively affect teaching and learning. It is important for mentors to use clear, precise language, with a rationale for *why* the observed aspect was effective.

Naming and elaborating upon successes is important because it helps the teacher have a balanced perspective of their teaching and helps them recognize and remember to continue to do the things that are making a positive impact in their classroom. It may also be an opportunity to deepen teachers' knowledge of teaching and learning. A mentor who notices that the teacher is cuing the students when they want a raised hand versus a choral response might write:

> I noticed that you provided a cue to students telling them how you wanted them to participate while signaling that everyone's active participation is needed. For example, you said, "I'm looking for a raised hand to tell me . . ."

and later, "Everyone, what is the answer to . . ." This sets students up for success by letting them know what is expected of them and that active participation helps students sustain their attention and can be good formative feedback for you.

In addition, mentors should look for those "quick win" moments, when a simple adjustment in the teacher's actions could positively affect students' learning and promoting equitable classroom spaces. For example, a mentor may notice that a group of students were off task during independent work time and that it appears that one student is initiating a side conversation. The mentor may write:

> I noticed that Table 4 was struggling to complete the task independently. You reminded them four times to get on task in 5 minutes, three of those were directed at [student]. It might be helpful to use proximity during directions and then immediately check in with [student] to see if they need any support or if the work is possibly not challenging [student] enough.

At times, a mentor may observe something during a drop-in that they want to follow up on with the teacher later. When that occurs, the mentor may add a "wondering," such as "I wonder if the students at Table 4 need more clarity on how to productively work interdependently [or if more differentiation might be needed]. Perhaps we can touch base on this." In this manner, feedback is presented as an invitation, not a directive. It can also provide teachers with an idea of a potential focus goal related to equitable, ambitious instruction. Drop-ins can also foster a teacher's trust in their mentor, as written feedback demonstrates that the mentor is supportive, not judgmental (see example and resource in Appendix B).

Like brief interactions, drop-ins can be particularly impactful at the beginning of the year when the mentor is trying to get the "lay of the land" and establish trust with the teacher—particularly with new teachers who may need additional support and help recognizing their own strengths. Throughout the year, drop-ins bridge regularly scheduled observations and debriefing sessions, helping new and veteran teachers negotiate ambitious instruction with the full support of their mentor. Drop-ins are also a way for mentors to foster knowledge of and relationships with students, which is a requisite for implementing other important mentoring practices such as demonstration and co-teaching (see Chapters 11 and 12).

FINAL THOUGHTS ON BRIEF INTERACTIONS

Brief interactions, including drop-ins, support relationship building, increase mentor responsiveness, and support teachers' ability to implement ambitious, equitable instruction. They are not a replacement for the more in-depth learning experiences that occur via spending regular, goal-focused time in classrooms (e.g., co-teaching, stepping in, collecting video, collecting data) and conducting subsequent debriefs. Rather, their value is in building mentors' contextual knowledge of their teachers' classrooms and students; establishing and maintaining teacher and mentor (and student) relationships; and demonstrating mentors' commitment to teachers' development. All of these are central to effective mentoring and the ability to draw widely across mentoring practices.

QUESTIONS FOR REFLECTION AND ACTION

1. Trust—among mentor, teacher, students, and administrators—is a critical element of mentoring. How do you see brief interactions supporting the building and sustaining of each of these relationships?
2. When you consider brief interactions, what are your initial reactions? Anything that stands out as particularly beneficial? Things that worry or concern you about brief interactions?
3. Do you currently use brief interactions in your mentoring?

    a. If yes, has it had an impact on your relationships and work with teachers? Did the list of suggested ways to implement brief interactions give you any new ideas to try?
    b. If no, how might you try to incorporate brief interactions into your future practice? Are there particular teachers with whom you think drop-ins might be beneficial? What might that look like?

Chapter Six

Co-Planning and Resource Supports

Helping Fill in the Gaps

I honestly did not realize that I would be spending so much time gathering resources, thinking through different ways that I can help a teacher, thinking through how to use these resources. As I'm trying to do things for teachers, I'm often learning about new curricular resources that I haven't used before. It is taking a lot of time and is really stretching me. It's all good, just not what I expected.—Joelle, first-year mentor

Among teachers' many responsibilities, lesson planning may be one of the most deceptively complex. Skillful lesson planning requires deep knowledge of learning standards; content and related pedagogical approaches; students' prior knowledge, interests, and learning needs; and a broad scope of instructional and curricular resources. Teachers must then be able to weave all of this into coherent, engaging, rigorous, and differentiated lessons that facilitate ambitious learning for all students. This is no simple task!

Lesson planning and the ability to draw upon and effectively use a range of professional resources, including and beyond what the school may provide, is also a high-stakes practice. It directly affects students' opportunities to learn and be meaningfully engaged in the classroom! While many mentors expect to support *new* teachers' planning, experienced teachers often also benefit from co-planning and resource support.

Co-planning occurs when a mentor and teacher share responsibility for developing a lesson, a portion of a lesson, or a series of lessons. Co-planning provides concrete and specific support to meet their goals for ambitious teaching and learning. It can also be a way for mentors to disrupt observed patterns of inequitable practice.

When co-planning, mentors may differentiate the support they offer depending on teachers' familiarity with what is being planned, including any instructional activities (IA) related to their goal and/or their needs. For example, when working with a teacher who is largely unfamiliar with an IA, such as analyzing data or literary text and facilitating student discussion around that analysis, the mentor may take the lead in planning. While they plan with the teacher they will likely *think aloud* as they plan, making visible the decision-making that informs their planning. A mentor might say:

> What I want to address with students in this lesson is how to ground their ideas in the text. To do this I will plan to first explain why and how to use evidence from a text to support my ideas and then I will model how to do it. Looking at the text, I will use the first paragraph as my model. Let's write out what to say to effectively explain and then model.

When teachers are more familiar with the planning related to an IA, mentors may focus on fostering joint decision-making. For example, a mentor might say:

> I could see a couple of different ways to get students to ground their ideas in the text (or data). For example, you could ask, "Help me see where you found that?"; "What in the text/data helped you come to that conclusion?"; or "Can you show us where you got this idea so we can all go to that section?" You could also make sure to name and note when students do reference the text/data. How do these sound? Would any of these ideas work for you and your students? Do you have another idea?

As teachers take up more responsibility for planning, mentors' support fades.

IDEAS FOR HOW AND WHEN TO CO-PLAN

There are many circumstances when a mentor and teacher might opt to co-plan. Occasionally, a teacher or administrator might directly ask the mentor to support with planning. More often co-planning flows from an existing mentoring focus. For example, a teacher may worry that too much instructional time is being lost due to off-task student behaviors.

During an observation, the mentor concurs that strategies to support a productive learning environment are needed. While at the same time, the mentor observes that the lesson lacks rigor and active student engagement. During the debrief, the mentor and teacher may discuss strategies to prevent and respond to off-task behavior *and* co-plan to increase rigor and embed more meaningful engagement opportunities.

In order to effectively co-plan, mentors must designate time to become familiar with their teachers' skills and specific areas of need related to co-planning, as well as their grade-level standards and available curricular resources. Regular observations and relationships with teachers help mentors gain the necessary knowledge to (co-)identify a logical starting point for co-planning that will likely yield the most immediate positive impact on student learning and engagement.

Mentors must also factor in the teachers' specific context. What are students' varying needs? Of the available materials, do they reflect current standards (e.g., NGSS, NCSS, CCSS)? Are the materials diversity responsive? With these factors in mind, there are many possible co-planning foci. Below are examples that are both common and impactful:

- Writing objectives to ensure rigor, purpose, and clarity, as well as why these matter
- Revising lessons to increase coherence (i.e., alignment among objective, assessment, and instruction)
- Developing clear, purposeful lesson openings and closings that help students focus on teaching points and their relevance
- Crafting student-friendly, clear, precise, and academically complex language for mini-lessons or other formats that require explicit instruction and modeling
- Designing rigorous questions or topics for discussion and, as needed, incorporating specific ways to disrupt patterns leading to inequitable outcomes for students
- Connecting content/concepts to real-world issues and examples to increase rigor, relevance, and motivation
- Expanding the teacher's pedagogic repertoire to include a range of active, purposeful, culturally responsive, evidence-based approaches to meaningfully engage *all* students
- Embedding principles of "universal design for learning" to support all learners
- Shifting from more teacher-centered to student-centered instruction that includes increasing student talk and active, meaningful engagement
- Building in processes and purposes for meaningful collaborative work so that students will take on more ownership of and responsibility for their own, and each other's, learning
- Ensuring readings, activities, and language are culturally sustaining and that the content is accurate and does not demonstrate bias (considering race, ethnicity, economic status, dis/ability status, gender, gender identity, religion, and more)
- Incorporating well-designed formative, and where appropriate summative, assessment to guide instruction during and after the lesson
- Building and sustaining a productive, equitable classroom environment to ensure the classroom is safe, both physically and for student intellectual

risk-taking. This may include addressing relationships, transitions, routines, and procedures

CO-PLANNING IN TANDEM WITH OTHER MENTORING PRACTICES

Co-planning can be used to address a wide range of planning-related teacher goals. Like other mentoring practices, co-planning should be used flexibly, responsively, and in tandem with other practices. For example, while co-planning, mentors may find it beneficial to use demonstrations and/or rehearsals (see Chapter 9).

After co-planning a lesson, mentors may schedule to observe that lesson, collecting targeted data (see Chapter 3) related back to the original goal (i.e., the reason for co-planning in the first place). If this is not possible, the pair may opt to video the lesson for later analysis (see Chapter 7). Some teachers may need additional scaffolding to successfully implement the co-planned lesson, and thus the mentor and teacher may co-teach (see Chapter 12) the lesson. The decision regarding which mentoring practices to use should be directly related to what the teacher needs in order to successfully implement the focal IA independently and responsively.

IDEAS FOR HOW AND WHEN TO PROVIDE RESOURCE SUPPORT

There are many scenarios where co-planning is a logical and appropriate choice for supporting teachers across their careers. However, it may not always be sufficient or the best choice to meet teachers' planning needs. Alongside co-planning, mentors may find that their teachers would benefit from *resource support* to more effectively use their existing curricular resources, to procure professional resources to fill curricular gaps, and/or to build teacher knowledge in relation to their goals.

Resource support can address a range of teachers' planning needs, beginning with building teachers' understanding of and ability to use new and existing curricular materials. For example, when presented with a new math curricular material, new *and* veteran teachers may need help making sense of and using these resources. Or perhaps a teacher's instruction would be even more robust and responsive if their mentor helped them explore the extension options provided. New and veteran teachers alike may also require support and knowledge building in response to standards (e.g., NGSS, NCSS, CCSS), new curricula (e.g., from core reading programs to inquiry-based science), new technology, or new-to-them IAs.

Another way mentors can offer resource support is by helping teachers address curriculum bias. For example, if the social studies curriculum the school adopted depicts westward expansion or the civil rights movement in ways that erase or sanitize experiences of people of color (and other people with marginalized identities), a mentor can help locate resources that augment the curriculum to provide a more historically accurate and nuanced perspective. In literature, mentors can help teachers select texts that center on a wide range of ethnic, socioeconomic, religious, LGBTQIA+, geographic, and dis/ability experiences.

Other times, teachers may want, or have, to incorporate a new IA. In these cases, mentors may locate and share resources that build teachers' background knowledge. For example, perhaps a primary teacher needs to implement a word wall because it is their goal or a building-wide expectation. A mentor will want to ensure that the teacher understands the purpose of word walls *and* all the steps of using them effectively so they become a useful classroom resource.

In this case, the mentor may identify and share professional readings on what word walls are, how they support literacy development, ways to select words, and engaging activities to get students to use the word wall. The mentor and teacher may read together during a debriefing session or read independently, discussing the readings during the next debrief. Then, perhaps the teacher is ready to move forward on their own implementing word walls in their classroom.

RESOURCE SUPPORT IN TANDEM WITH OTHER MENTORING PRACTICES

During or after offering resource support, mentors will draw from the full array of mentoring practices to ensure teachers can independently use the resources reviewed. For example, in the word wall example above, the mentor and teacher may decide to co-plan a lesson, introducing the first contributions to the word wall.

Another mentor may opt to demonstrate and have the teacher rehearse the introduction of a word wall during the debrief (see Chapter 9). Follow-up, then, may include observations to collect data and perhaps step in (see Chapters 3 and 10) or co-teach (see Chapter 12). Afterward, the mentor would facilitate a subsequent debrief to help the teacher further refine the principled use of word walls in ways that support and empower students.

BUILDING AND EXPANDING MENTORS' KNOWLEDGE FOR TEACHING AND LEARNING

The knowledge base for providing equitable, ambitious instruction for all students is constantly evolving. This in turn means that on top of developing their knowledge and practice base around mentoring, mentors' knowledge base and practices related to teaching must also continuously develop. Further adding to mentors' already steep learning curve is the fact that many mentors work with teachers in grade levels and disciplines that differ from their own experiences and expertise.

To mentor effectively, and especially to co-plan or provide resource support, mentors need continuous designated time, support, and access to resources that build their knowledge and capacity, as well as help them keep abreast of the changes happening related to teaching and learning. This may include building knowledge and familiarizing themselves with

- relevant grade-level and content-area standards (e.g., CCSS, NGSS, NCSS);
- developmentally appropriate, culturally responsive, evidence-based pedagogy;
- new IAs and pedagogical approaches; and
- curricular review of the materials teachers use in order to understand how it is structured, how it does (and does not) align to standards, and the extent to which it is (or is not) culturally relevant and sustaining in content, principles, and practices (see Gay, 2018; Ladson-Billings, 2014; Paris, 2012).

The amount of time mentors must invest to learn, understand, and apply each largely depends on their own previous experiences with and knowledge of the context and content. Still, mentors, and mentoring programs, should anticipate the need to invest substantial time bolstering knowledge and ensure that time is allocated to continuous learning about teaching.

FINAL THOUGHTS ABOUT CO-PLANNING AND PROCURING RESOURCES

Co-planning and resource support help teachers realize their ambitious instructional goals. These practices can make the nuances of planning clearer and more concrete, resulting in more effective teaching and learning. Co-planning and resource support also ensure teachers' practices are informed by a deeper knowledge base related to content, pedagogy, and equitable, ambitious instruction. When used in tandem with other practices, as part of a larger mentoring cycle, mentors can facilitate observable and impactful changes to new and veteran teachers' ability to effectively serve *all* their students.

QUESTIONS FOR REFLECTION AND ACTION

1. Have you ever co-planned with a teacher? What went well? What were the challenges? Based on these experiences, what next steps could you take to maximize the potential of this practice?
2. If co-planning has not been part of your mentoring, how might the information in this chapter help you weave co-planning into your repertoire?
3. Are there resources or content shifts (e.g., CCSS, NGSS, NCSS) where you feel you need additional knowledge and support? Which mentors, teachers, administrators, and professional organizations might be potential sources of that knowledge and support?
4. Have you ever found yourself in a situation where a teacher needed support in using curricular resources and/or building their knowledge base? How might the information from this chapter help you in your work with teachers? How might you differentiate your approach when working with novice or more experienced teachers?
5. Explore one or more of these resources, and consider how they could be integrated as resource supports for teachers or your colleagues: Zinn Education Project, Teaching Tolerance, Social Justice Books a Teaching for Change Project, and Assessing Bias in Standards and Curricular Materials.
6. Think about the teachers you work with currently. Which one might be most amenable to or benefit from co-planning and/or resource supports? What are their specific needs, and how do those needs relate to their goals? What would you want the teacher's role to be for planning and during instruction? What additional mentoring practices might you incorporate (or be curious about incorporating) to help them transition to independent, ambitious teaching?

Chapter Seven

Video Analysis

Visual Support for Teacher Growth

I need examples. Video helps me see all the pieces: the way I ask a question, how students are engaged, the tone I use, the way I'm positioned that maybe the students can't see. So many different little things that matter a lot. It's made a huge impact seeing it for myself and discussing it with my mentor.— Monique, teacher

Video is right there without bias attached. A teacher is able to see what they are actually doing while they are teaching. It holds the data within a real-life example.—Rashid, third-year instructional coach

When teachers set goals for trying out new instructional activities (IAs), or improving upon IAs they have been implementing, there are times when the best course forward is for the mentor to *show* an IA to the teacher. Video analysis is one of several mentoring practices that can accomplish this aim.

Video analysis is a versatile, collaborative practice that provides teachers with a visual representation of an IA related to their goals for improving instruction. The video may be of the teacher themselves, another teacher, the mentor, or an exemplar from an outside source. The analysis of the video can focus on identifying places for improvement in current levels of performance, or in the case of an exemplar, provide teachers with a model of skillful implementation of an IA.

As the mentor and teacher view the video together, they can stop and/or rewatch a segment at any point to analyze and discuss what they are seeing in the implementation of the IA. They can stop to note effective instructional elements, and *why* it was effective, as well as brainstorm adjustments that could be made to maximize impact of the IA or where a different "teacher move" may be equally or more impactful and why.

Generally, one of three scenarios drives the decision to use video analysis:

1. A teacher is struggling to implement an IA (or element of).
2. The mentoring focus is potentially sensitive, such as the teacher's tone, demeanor, and/or practices toward students or a group of students.
3. The mentor is introducing or reviewing a complex IA (or element of) that is best explained through a visual representation.

The first two situations may be best addressed by collecting video footage of the teacher. Alternatively, the mentor and teacher may decide that a video of another teacher or mentor demonstrating skilled implementation of the IA might be the preferred next step, or a step prior to videotaping the teacher. The third situation typically calls for an exemplar video of another teacher, and/or one of the additional visually oriented, more highly scaffolded practices such as collegial visits, demonstration teaching, or co-teaching (discussed in Chapters 8, 11, and 12, respectively).

THINGS TO CONSIDER BEFORE VIDEO ANALYSIS OF A TEACHER'S PRACTICE

Having a teacher view a video of their own instruction has distinct advantages. No matter how careful mentors are when collecting observational data, it is still filtered through their eyes. Video on the other hand can capture teachers' instruction and students' responses or how students engage with each other and the content without being filtered through another's lens.

No matter how observant a teacher is, as they teach, they are making a multitude of decisions and cannot be aware of everything at once. Videos show teachers exactly what is happening across the classroom. Replaying videos can help teachers have a more encompassing depiction of what is happening in their classroom in relation to their goals.

Even so, mentors should be aware of some potential challenges and considerations related to capturing video of the teacher's own instruction. Key among them is that video self-analysis may put the teacher in a vulnerable position. This is particularly true if the mentoring focus is on an especially sensitive part of a teacher's practice, such as tone or equitable practices. However, mentors can proactively address these concerns with careful planning and communication.

Mentors can begin by evaluating their relationship with the teacher and assessing the teacher's disposition toward being videoed. Are they excited? Nervous? Worried? This information is invaluable to helping make sure the video experience is positive and productive. Mentors should listen carefully and address teachers' concerns. If teachers are reluctant, mentors can ease them into this practice by analyzing videos of the mentor or another teacher while demonstrating their nonjudgmental, problem-solving, and collaborative stance.

Another way mentors can mitigate concerns and maintain honest communication is by establishing agreed-upon guidelines for capturing and reviewing the video that include

- stating that the video is for *only* the teacher's and mentor's eyes;
- explaining that the purpose of the video is to learn from practice, not to judge;
- being explicit about where the mentor will/will not be when the video is being recorded;
- determining how to prepare students for the video so that the experience is minimally disruptive and demonstrates that the teacher is also a learner (e.g., Why is video being taken? How will video be used? Will the recording device be moved about the classroom and zoom in on students and their work?); and
- deciding on an opt-in/opt-out protocol if the teacher or students are having an "off" day during the video recording.

On this last point, there is no "one right" answer. One option is to continue recording and adjust the debrief to focus on the elements of practice contributing to the "off" day. For example, the mentor and teacher can discuss strategies for preventing and/or responding to similar challenges in the future.

A second option is to have a "cut sign" that indicates the recording should be stopped. The mentor can then shift to an alternate practice such as collecting data and/or stepping in (see Chapters 3 and 10). The debrief would then focus on the data collected and/or insights gained from how and why the mentor stepped in, not video analysis. Depending on the teacher's preference, the video would be deleted or given to the teacher for potential future analysis.

When weighing the risks associated with videotaping, particularly the potential for an "off day," there is a final important consideration. On one hand, much can be learned from lessons that do not go well, making even this experience potentially beneficial for the teacher.

Yet, relationships are central to mentoring. If teachers firmly believe that mentors are their advocates and collaborators, not their judges, they will be more likely to open their practice—even on their worst days—to video with their mentor. Mentors can demonstrate their respect by being responsive to teachers' needs and preferences. If being videotaped stresses a teacher to the point where they are not open to learning or if it is negatively affecting their ability to teach, then it is not worth it at that moment.

VIEWING AND ANALYZING VIDEOS OF A TEACHER'S PRACTICE

Once the choice to videotape in the teacher's own classroom has been made, the mentor must determine, based on the teacher's goals, what aspect of the lesson they should capture. This may be a full lesson, a single component, and/or a series of clips that are central to depicting the teacher's goal. While seeing themselves and their students in action will be informative, the biggest impact will come from the analysis of the video during the debrief.

To prepare for viewing and debriefing the video, mentors should consider what it is *specifically* that the teacher needs to see and analyze. Mentors may find it helpful to trim the video and identify specific time stamps to view with the teacher. This simply leaves more time for analysis by eliminating any viewing that is not central to the goal. Mentors might also choose to add annotations directly to the video, either through whispered comments while recording such as "Pay close attention to the language you use here" or by adding written notes to specific points, with time stamps indicated, after recording.

At some point shortly after the video is captured, ideally that same day or at least within 24–48 hours, mentors and teachers will debrief to analyze the video and determine their next steps. Teachers may have preferences about the initial video viewing that mentors should honor. Some teachers may prefer to view the video privately, before viewing and analyzing it with their mentor. For other teachers, viewing the video on their own may be a daunting task that they wish to avoid, and they may prefer to just watch it with their mentor. Mentors who know each of their teachers are able to provide more responsive mentoring based on this knowledge.

Mentors also need an advance plan for facilitating video review and analysis. Mentors may find it effective to plan for and implement the same discussion protocol, as well as language stems and questions, discussed in Chapter 4:

> "In relationship to the goal and what you see in this video, what is working well? Why is this effective practice? How does it support student learning?"
> "What are some challenges? What might be modeled, practiced, or discussed to facilitate meaningful change to teaching and learning?"

"What are the teacher's next steps?"

"What steps can the mentor take to support . . . ?"

This keeps the discussion in familiar terrain and maintains focus on the instructional goal.

Mentors can also suggest that the teacher collect data while viewing the video (see Chapter 3). Data collection should focus on data related directly to the mentoring goal. Mentors will likely need to support teachers to collect accurate and useful data.

Also, much like in a debriefing session based on data collection, mentors may need a plan to refocus the teacher's attention back to the instructional goal. Videos provide a broad view of the classroom that teachers are not privy to while teaching (i.e., there is a lot to notice!), and some redirection back to the goal may be needed. In addition, many teachers are often overly self-critical. To help teachers have a balanced perspective on their instruction, mentors should be prepared to identify aspects of the IA that the teacher did well and how that aspect was effective in supporting student learning. In either of these situations, one clear benefit of capturing practice through video is that videos can be replayed, providing an opportunity for deeper analysis.

VIEWING AND ANALYZING EXEMPLAR VIDEOS

Exemplar videos are another excellent resource for visually representing instructional activities. For example, imagine a teacher learned about document-based questioning (DBQ) from a respected colleague but wants to see DBQ in action before implementation in their classroom. Or perhaps the teacher taught one or more DBQ lessons and wants to see how to further enhance their teaching or address challenges related to implementation. Exemplar videos can be obtained from a number of sources, including another teacher, a mentor, or on sites like the Teaching Channel, High Leverage Practice from the CEEDAR Center for special education, Teaching Works at University of Michigan, and Annenberg Learner.

When mentors identify exemplar videos, they need to prepare to facilitate learning by reviewing the entire video and thinking through the following:

- What are the teacher's specific needs?
- What critical features should be highlighted (e.g., wait time, follow-up questions to deepen discussion)?
- Would it be helpful for the teacher to collect data as it relates to the goal during the initial viewing? If so, the mentor should have a couple of options for data collection in mind to present to the teacher for their consideration.

- What principles related to effective instruction do teachers need to understand so they can make their own informed decisions and adaptations after viewing the video?
- How can the mentor help the teacher concretize what they viewed and analyze and use those insights to prepare for their own classroom application?

There are several benefits to exemplar videos. Teachers see effective classroom practices implemented. They can rewatch portions as needed. Teachers and mentors can pause to discuss elements that make the IA effective and how to make principled adaptations to meet the needs of their students. The teacher and mentor may pause the video and demonstrate or rehearse portions of the lesson (more on this in Chapter 9). An additional potential benefit to using such videos is that they often include commentary and/or resources from the teacher or other experts in the field.

Yet, mentors should bear in mind the limitations of videos drawn from contexts other than the teacher's classroom. In particular, teachers may be tempted to say something like, "but my students can't . . . ," potentially revealing internalized biases or the need for additional forms of mentored support. Mentors can prepare probing questions to get at the heart of such statements and then respond in principled and effective ways. For example, mentors might begin by saying, "I hear you saying your students do not currently do [x]; can you tell me a bit more about that? What would it take to support them to be able to . . . ?" Or perhaps, "What are you seeing that suggests they cannot [x]? What do you think is preventing [x], and what can we do to address that need?"

If bias is revealed, often in the form of low expectations, mentors may need to be prepared to explicitly name and challenge negative unconscious (or conscious) beliefs about students. Also, mentors may want to raise teachers' expectations for what their students can achieve by suggesting demonstration teaching (see Chapter 11) or co-teaching (see Chapter 12). These practices can provide visual "proof" of what students are capable of when given the appropriate supports. If teacher knowledge and skill or lack of access to resources is the central issue, mentors can address that concern through co-planning and resource support (see Chapter 6), collegial visits (see Chapter 8), or demonstration teaching (see Chapter 11) or co-teaching (see Chapter 12).

A final important caveat, related to any form of video analysis, is not to get the teacher to imitate the model in the video. Rather, video should be used to help the teacher understand and apply principled adaptations of the IA in their own classroom contexts.

VIDEO ANALYSIS IN TANDEM WITH OTHER MENTORING PRACTICES

Using video analysis in conjunction with demonstration teaching (see Chapter 11) or co-teaching (see Chapter 12) can be an effective interweaving of practices. Plus, it can ultimately provide an exemplar video for the mentor's library of resources. When a mentor is willing to be recorded, this not only provides opportunities for shared review and all the benefits of video analysis but also can build trust through the mentor's modeled vulnerability.

There are also a wide range of next steps that can be taken based on any type of video analysis and debrief! It may make sense for mentors to co-plan a lesson (see Chapter 6), facilitate a collegial visit (see Chapter 8), observe and collect data (see Chapter 3), co-teach (see Chapter 12), or return to videotape again. There are as many options as there are mentoring practices discussed. The key is that the video analysis is used within a broader mentoring cycle that flexibly and responsively integrates inside/outside practices to further teachers' progress toward their own goals and toward achieving more ambitious classroom practices.

FINAL THOUGHTS ON VIDEO ANALYSIS

Video analysis is a versatile tool with many benefits. To obtain the most positive impact from video, and to proactively address potential limitations, mentors need to be thoughtful and intentional through all phases: selecting videos, facilitating analysis and learning, and identifying additional inside/outside practices to support teachers to independent practice.

How this unfolds will look different with each teacher. After all, responsiveness and teacher centeredness are core to educative mentoring, and video analysis is no exception. The principles and guidelines discussed in this chapter are the foundation for mentor decision-making and making the most of this mentoring practice.

QUESTIONS FOR REFLECTION AND ACTION

1. Have you ever used video analysis? What went well? What were the challenges? What are some ways you could be preemptive in addressing challenges before, during, or after video analysis in future use?
2. What platforms have you used for recording, preparing, sharing, and archiving videos?
3. Or if you have not used a specific platform, the following are tools for video analysis. Explore one or more to consider if/how you might use them: Big Blue Button, Zoom, and Google Hangouts. Some applica-

tions such as OneNote and Apple Pencil allow you to annotate in real time, while CloudApp, MediaNotes, and TouchCast Studio allow you to annotate after the fact.

4. If you have not been regularly using video analysis, how might the information in this chapter help you weave video analysis into your repertoire? Or if video analysis is or has been in your repertoire, are there any insights from this chapter that could help you augment or fine-tune what you are already doing?

5. We suggested some sources for videos such as the Teaching Channel, CEEDAR, Teaching Works (University of Michigan), and Annenberg Learner. If you have not explored these sites, try one and see what you think—is this a resource that could be helpful to one or more of the teachers with whom you work? If you have used them or other similar sites, what were the benefits and challenges?

6. Are there other sources for high-quality videos you would recommend to your colleagues?

7. Think about the teachers you work with currently. Consider both video analysis of *their own practice* and/or *exemplars*:

   a. Which one might be most amenable to or benefit from video analysis? How might you approach this teacher? What would you want the teacher's role to be for planning and during instruction?

   b. Who might be most resistant? How might you approach this teacher? What steps might you take to increase their comfort and readiness with the video analysis process?

Chapter Eight

Collegial Visits

Learning From Peers

One of my special educators, "Felicity," felt so isolated and discouraged. She was struggling to establish centers, but it felt too big. We had co-planned, but she had rushed through to an end product, had not taken sufficient time to teach each center topic or the process for how to work in centers. Not surprisingly, it fell apart. I took her to see a teacher in a different building, and it reinspired her. She saw what was possible, could talk to the teacher about how much work it took to establish centers, but how and why it was worth it in the long run. The host also shared several centers materials, which helped her feel ready to try again. Felicity ended up making centers a structure in both reading and math and loved the time working with small groups *and* seeing students grow in their independent skills!—Nadia, fourth-year mentor

The ultimate aim of educative mentoring is to support teachers in enacting ambitious instruction. As the name suggests, ambitious instruction is complex and involves many components that must all be woven together in a responsive and equity-oriented ways. It is perhaps not surprising, then, that in order to be responsive to their teachers' needs, mentors must be able to select from and enact a broad repertoire of mentoring practices.

As discussed in the prior chapter, responsive mentoring may include using a visual model coupled with a debriefing session to help teachers better understand an instructional activity (IA) reflective of their goal. Collegial visits are another option for providing a visual model that also has the added benefit of potentially broadening teachers' professional network.

In a *collegial visit*, the teacher and mentor co-observe in the classroom of a purposefully selected colleague who provides a model of exemplary practice related to the mentoring goal. The visit can occur in the teacher's own or another school. Then, as in all mentoring practices, a debrief follows the co-observation to build and deepen knowledge, as well as identify a path to help the teacher successfully take up the IA in their own classroom.

WHEN AND WHY TO IMPLEMENT COLLEGIAL VISITS

Collegial visits can occur at any point in a mentoring cycle and can support teachers' implementation of nearly any IA. However, due to the time and logistical considerations, collegial visits are most beneficial for implementing complex IAs that are not readily explored through discussion or reading. For example, perhaps a teacher wants to implement literature circles for the first time but would first like to see what student-led discussions look like and how they are facilitated. A collegial visit provides an opportunity to see an IA skillfully implemented with students prior to the teacher trying it out in their own classroom.

A collegial visit also allows the teacher to see more of the classroom than what is displayed in videos. For one, the observation is completely unedited. Also, coming into a classroom provides the teacher with an opportunity to collect a broader range of data related to their goal. For example, the visiting teacher can listen in and observe smaller groups or step back and observe the entire class at any given time. Relatedly, a collegial visit helps the teacher see all the materials in the room related to the IA, such as any anchor charts, where and how materials are organized, and so on.

A unique benefit of collegial visits is the opportunity for teachers to leave their classrooms and, in some cases, their school to observe and potentially talk to other educators. Teachers rarely get opportunities to observe colleagues' classrooms, and these observations can expand teachers' perspectives. A collegial visit also introduces a teacher to a like-minded colleague who may become a professional resource.

HOW TO IMPLEMENT COLLEGIAL VISITS

The following steps pave the path for a successful collegial visit. First and foremost, mentors must make sure this practice is the best choice at this time. This involves weighing out the teacher's goals and preferences, as well as the benefits, potential challenges, and consequences of collegial visits compared to other practices that might be suitable.

Mentors must also assess the availability of a strong model of this particular IA. For example, if the visit is to show a visual representation of a teacher effectively implementing literature circles, mentors must know another teacher who is experienced and skillful with this IA. It is also helpful to schedule visits in similar grade levels whenever possible.

Once the decision is made to pursue a collegial visit, logistics need to be addressed. To start, principal(s) need to be informed, sanction the visit, and provide classroom coverage. At the same time, mentors need to coordinate with the host teacher to discuss purpose, dates, and times.

If possible, mentors should build in time for the visiting and host teachers to discuss before and/or after the observation. Busy schedules may make this challenging, but the visiting teacher will probably want to ask questions or even problem-solve with a colleague who shares, and is further along, in implementing the focus IA. The collegial visit shows the class at one specific point in time. Therefore, the visiting teacher might want to ask about the structures that helped students engage in insightful, text-based, student-led, and inclusive discussion, as well as how those structures were selected and established over time.

PREPARING FOR THE VISIT

When entering another teacher's room, it is natural for the visiting teacher to want to see everything. Prior to the visit, the visiting teacher and mentor should identify a clear focus and data collection plan. On which specific aspects of the IA will the visiting teacher take notes? To gather targeted data focused on the IA, will the visiting teacher use a specific data collection tool? Will the visiting teacher sit back and observe the whole class, sit in with one group for the entire time, or move about groups? There are many choices for data collection tools, and referring to Chapter 3 beforehand may be helpful. Once tentatively decided, the mentor should communicate these ideas to the host teacher in advance to gain their consent.

Right before the observation, the mentor and visiting teacher should pre-brief to reinforce the purpose, review the observational plan, and address any other questions. It is also helpful to talk about having a "generosity of spirit" toward the host teacher, who is human and is engaging in a potentially vulnerable action by opening their practice to observers. Mentors should guide visiting teachers to recognize this and focus on being quick to observe, collect data, and generate questions, while being slow to draw conclusions or pass judgment.

Co-observation by teacher *and* mentor is critical. Classrooms are complex spaces, and mentors should also be ready to facilitate meaning-making of any unexpected occurrences during the observation. Mentors may consider collecting data using the same protocol that the teacher is using in order to compare and discuss during the debrief, and/or generate potential debriefing questions or points of conversation based on what is observed.

DEBRIEFING THE VISIT

A debrief should happen soon after the observation, ideally immediately after, or at least within 24–48 hours. As in any debrief, the intent is to co-analyze data, discuss and deconstruct (i.e., identify essential elements and discuss their importance) the observed practice, and create actionable next steps. To frame this discussion, a slightly modified three-part version of the debriefing protocol outlined in Chapter 4 is suggested:

Identify Successes

"What effectively supported [implementation of IA related to goal]?"

Mentors should ensure this discussion includes an exploration of "why" specific actions were effective, through specific data that were collected and/or "teacher moves" they observed that supported successful implementation. This is an opportunity to make complexities of the IA concrete by highlighting the areas in which the host teacher's instruction, or even aspects of the classroom environment such as materials storage or anchor charts, can serve as a model.

Identify Change Opportunities

"Given what you observed and experienced in this classroom, what are some of the changes you might want to make to move closer to your goal?"

Based on these reflections, connecting back to specifics observed, the mentor and teacher should work collaboratively to facilitate meaningful change to the teacher's practice. This entails an analysis of where the teacher wants to be in their practice, where they are now, what sequence of steps are needed to get from "here to there," and how what they just observed can support that progression.

Determine Next Steps to Continue the Mentoring Cycle

"Of these possible steps, which one seems to be the best choice for now? Why? What exactly will that look like? What do you need to do? What can I do?"

Based on the opportunities for change, the teacher and mentor determine next steps for both parties. To do this, mentors and teachers should draw from the full repertoire of inside/outside practices to ensure the teacher has a clear plan with support for successful, independent implementation of the IA.

For example, sometimes a teacher will be ready to implement the practice on their own or after co-planning with their mentor (see Chapter 6). Then, the next step is for the teacher to attempt, while the mentor schedules an observation, to collect data on implementation, or possibly even video-record (see

Chapter 7) for later analysis with the teacher. Or perhaps the teacher needs more scaffolding and the mentor may demonstration teach next (see Chapter 11). Or maybe the most logical next step is for the mentor and teacher to co-plan and possibly co-teach (see Chapter 12). There are any number of ways to support the teacher to independence, and those should be decided on together.

Leaving Out "What Were the Challenges?"

Missing from this modified protocol is identifying challenges. This omission is recommended for three reasons. First, the purpose of a collegial visit is *not* to evaluate the host teacher's practice or to provide mentoring to that teacher. The focus is on learning from the host teacher's effective implementation. Second, as the debrief is between the visiting teacher and mentor, the host teacher is not present to identify and redress areas of challenge, and therefore, it is best to avoid opening that conversation. And third, in keeping with a spirit of generosity, the host teacher has put themselves into a vulnerable space by opening their practice to observation and conversation. It is important to honor that in the debrief.

Worth noting, in rare instances, is that an observation may not go well for a range of reasons, some of which may be beyond the control of the host teacher. If such a situation arises, it may warrant some nonjudgmental, solutions-oriented discussion between the mentor and visiting teacher. In these cases, it is best to acknowledge the problematic practice, ensure that follow-up with the host will occur if needed, such as in cases of student safety and well-being, and then redirect the conversation back to the observation focus.

CONSIDERING AND ADDRESSING NEGATIVE OR UNINTENDED CONSEQUENCES

Collegial visits allow teachers to see complex IAs implemented successfully in front of students. Entering a new space and observing a colleague's practice is a break from routine that can spark additional perspectives and be reinvigorating. Viewing how a different set of students responds to instruction can further broaden perspectives. Additionally, teachers can potentially follow-up with the person who taught the lesson to ask questions, problem-solve, and expand their professional network.

As with any mentoring practice, it is important to proactively think through the potential challenges and unintended consequences that may occur. While rare, the following issues may arise, and advanced awareness makes it easier to respond productively in the moment:

What Happens If the Observed Lesson Does Not Go Well?

Even the most skilled educators have "off" days and lessons that do not go as well as they would hope. Mentors can prepare the visiting teacher for this by setting a tone of "generosity of spirit" from the start. Then they can work with the visiting teacher, and possibly later with the host, to examine an "ineffective" lesson as a teachable moment, co-reflecting and co-generating ideas for responding to challenges observed.

What Happens If the Lesson Goes Too Well and the Visiting Teacher Feels Discouraged?

It is possible that a visiting teacher may see the observed practice as out of their reach. Mentors can respond in a variety of ways:

- Asking for additional information about what their teacher is struggling with
- Recentering on the singular observation focus
- Shifting the conversation to identify concrete and immediate next steps the teacher may take to grow their practice
- Guiding their own thinking about next steps with the teacher to include more intentional scaffolding such as co-planning (see Chapter 6), demonstrations and rehearsals (see Chapter 9), and/or demonstration (see Chapter 11) and co-teaching (see Chapter 12) in the teacher's classroom.

What If Teachers Just Treat It Like a Break From Teaching Rather Than a Learning Experience?

Prior to the collegial visit mentors should ensure that their teacher is committed to the goal of implementing the IA that is the focus of the visit. This will increase the likelihood the teacher is fully invested in learning from the event. Having the mentor beside them with a clear focus/data collection tool for the observation will likely also help.

What If the Teacher Makes Excuses About Why This Would Never Work in Their Classroom?

Matching the classroom by as many characteristics as possible can reduce the chances that comments like "Well, my students . . ." will happen. As discussed in Chapter 7, mentors should prepare follow-up questions to understand what beliefs or misunderstandings underlie that statement. Does the teacher hold biases that manifest in low expectations? Is the teacher unsure of their ability to move forward effectively? With a clearer understanding of the meaning behind the words, mentors can offer additional supports such as co-planning (see Chapter 6), demonstrations and rehearsals (see Chapter 9), demonstration teaching (see Chapter 11), and co-teaching (see Chapter 12).

What If the Observing Teacher Is Hypercritical of the Experience and/or the Teacher They Observed?

Mentors may opt to probe for more understanding, redirect the conversation back to the focus, and/or address the need for a "spirit of generosity." This may also be a situation where mentors are called upon to be models of professionalism and emphasize norms of professional discourse.

FINAL THOUGHTS ON COLLEGIAL VISITS

Collegial visits make IAs concrete and observable in unfiltered real time with real students by more skilled and experienced teachers. The vital debrief that follows further builds teachers' knowledge *of* and *for* their practice, bridging the gap from teachers learning *about* an IA to successful *independent application*. Furthermore, collegial visits can connect educators who have similar goals for, and likely beliefs about, teaching. These connections can be a source of ongoing support and learning.

QUESTIONS FOR REFLECTION AND ACTION

1. Have you ever facilitated a collegial visit? What went well? What were the challenges? Are there any insights from this chapter that could help you augment or fine-tune what you are already doing?
2. When you consider facilitating a collegial visit, what is your initial reaction? Are there things you find exciting about this practice? Things that make you uncertain or uncomfortable? How might the information in this chapter help you weave collegial visits into your repertoire?
3. Think about the teachers you currently mentor. Which ones might be most amenable to or benefit from *going on a* collegial visit? How might you approach this teacher? What might you want that teacher to focus on, and how would you go about preparing them (i.e., what to look for and how to collect data) to ensure the most meaningful experience?
4. Think about the teachers you mentor or who are in your professional networks:

   a. What are their instructional strengths?
   b. Who might be willing to host a collegial visit?

   c. How might you approach them and frame this mentoring practice?

   d. Taking Questions 3 and 4 together, can you think of any potential matches?

Chapter Nine

Demonstrations and Rehearsals

Ensuring Teachers Feel Ready to Teach

I had an "ah-ha" moment when talking to a principal. He had just come from a classroom observation and was so frustrated. He kept saying, "I told her to stop being so controlling during discussions. It's always ask a question, a student answers, she responds. Repeat! She never lets them talk to or build off each other." I said, "Does she know how to facilitate a whole class discussion in this way?" He said, "Well I told her how to do it." And I remember thinking, imagine if we said that about a student, "I told them to find evidence," but we never actually showed them how, explained why supporting ideas with evidence matters, never actually verified that they had what they needed to find evidence. We would be remiss to blame the students in this case. And we are remiss if we blame teachers without first teaching them and verifying they have the skills, mindsets, and tools to implement a practice.—Nadia, fourth-year mentor

The debrief is the heart of educative mentoring. It is a dedicated space for mentors and teachers to set instructional goals, analyze data collected during observations, problem-solve, reflect, and ultimately, collaborate to support teachers' independent implementation of ambitious instruction for all students. It is this last piece, cultivating teachers' ability to integrate their learning directly into their classroom practice, that is the essential aim of the debrief (see Chapter 4).

Demonstrations and/or *rehearsals* are two responsive practices that mentors can employ to facilitate meaningful change to teacher practice during the debrief. Both mentoring practices eliminate ambiguities that hinder teachers' goal attainment while building teachers' knowledge, pedagogic skills, and even confidence. While demonstrations and rehearsals work well in tandem, for the sake of clarity, they will be discussed separately in this chapter.

Demonstrations can occur "inside" the action of teaching when students are present (see Chapter 11) or "outside" the action of teaching, usually during the debrief. This chapter explores demonstrations "outside." Demonstrations "outside" provide the opportunity for a mentor to model all or part of an instructional activity (IA), and then co-engage with teachers in analysis and problem solving. Rehearsals serve a similar role, but instead of the mentor modeling, it is the teacher who leads the IA. Throughout the rehearsal, mentors and teachers co-analyze how to transition from the rehearsal to classroom instruction.

IMPLEMENTING DEMONSTRATIONS TO SUPPORT TEACHERS' INDEPENDENT PRACTICE

By its very name, ambitious instruction is, well, ambitious. IAs that reflect ambitious instruction include many components, each of which serves important functions. Without understanding the components and their purpose, teachers will have difficulty effectively implementing the IA in ways that are responsive to students' strengths and needs.

Therefore, when mentors use demonstrations during the debrief, they need to "unpack" (or *decompose*) the IA into its components. The purpose of decomposing is to identify the less observable and nuanced aspects of the IA that could be missed, and that are essential to effective implementation. Then after breaking down the IA into its components, mentors *recompose* the elements to reflect of full complexity of the IA, reinforcing the thinking and decision-making that occurs when enacting that IA (see Grossman et al., 2009). This reintegration is essential to support purposeful, adaptive practice, rather than thinking of the IA as being composed of items on a checklist.

To illustrate, suppose a mentor and a teacher are working on improving the teacher's facilitation of whole-group discussion. The teacher is looking to increase student participation, have students build off of and reference one another's thinking, and draw upon data, text, images, or other materials. During the debrief, if it seems that the teacher is unclear of exactly how to achieve their goal and conduct a productive class discussion, either the teacher or the mentor may choose to initiate a demonstration. At this point, mentors will need to stop and think about what goes into skilled, responsive discussion facilitation. Considerations must include

- the component parts that go into fostering a productive discussion;
- why each of those parts is necessary/how they contribute to the success of the IA;

- what the mentor knows about the students, the content currently being taught, and the related standards/expectations for ambitious instruction; and
- which component(s) should be modeled. It may be the entire IA as described below, or just a portion that best reflects the teacher's needs.

With all this in mind, the demonstration unfolds following the pattern of *model and identify* and *support transfer through shared meaning-making and application* with each component. Then, the mentor and teacher *recompose* (i.e., bring the IA back together in its entirety) *and discuss*. At any time during the demonstration, either the teacher or the mentor can pause (i.e., call for "time out") for more problem solving and discussion.

To illustrate this pattern, the following example of a mentor modeling a facilitated discussion is provided. While classroom discussions (or any other IA) do not unfold in purely linear ways, for the sake of shared clarity, the example below is organized sequentially as much as possible. To start, a mentor could provide an overview of the different components to give the full picture. For example:

> As you know, facilitating effective whole class discussions that get students to attend and respond to each other's ideas, rather than responding just to the teacher, and support their thinking with [data, text or visual evidence, etc.] is really complex! Now, I'm not trying to simplify this process, but to start it can help by just unpacking and thinking through all the necessary parts that go into facilitating a discussion. So, let's think together what these are. Before we even start, we have to think about how we might initiate the class discussion to pique students' interests. Then, we need to think about the language and instructional "moves" we use to facilitate discussion and orient students to each other and [data, text, etc.]. Finally, we need to think about how we'll close the discussion to deepen learning.

Then, depending on the teacher's need, the mentor could model one, some, or all of the components. Actually, demonstrating the IA would proceed as follows:

- *Model and identify (the first component) of the IA.* Mentor demonstrates how they frame the discussion (e.g., set the purpose, make expectations for participation explicit), by using the exact language and body positioning they would with a class. The mentor pauses during modeling to name and identify important nuances. For example, they might say, "Here I am framing the discussion for students . . ." or "Notice how I opened the lesson by . . ." Mentors then discuss *why* it is important to do this for and with students.

- *Transfer through shared meaning-making and application.* The teacher and mentor may generate ideas for how the teacher might frame a discussion in their own class, being very specific in identifying the language, routines, procedures, and so forth that lead to successful implementation.

This same process shared above, model and identify, and transfer through shared meaning-making and application, would repeat until all components, or the components the teacher wants to focus on, were addressed.

In the final step, *recompose and discuss*, the mentor models and/or summarizes the process as a whole and then asks the teacher to step back and reflect on the IA as a whole. Mentors might ask something like, "Facilitating discussions is a complex and important IA. What are you taking away from this demonstration? What do you see or understand a little differently now? In what ways will this demonstration influence your planning and teaching?"

TIPS FOR MAKING DEMONSTRATIONS EVEN MORE RESPONSIVE

When enacting a demonstration, it is important that the teacher is an active participant. As the example above is intended to illustrate, demonstrations are not simply mentor modeling, although modeling is important. Demonstrations should be dynamic with teachers interjecting and having the ownership to pause, problem-solve, and contextualize what was demonstrated to their personal style and their classroom, while maintaining the principles that undergird the IA. To this end mentors and teachers are encouraged to

- pause the demonstration to initiate discussion, highlight important aspects or components of the IA, reveal decision-making, and/or foster problem solving and connections to the teacher's classrooms;
- ask for part or the entire demonstration to be reenacted for added clarity or to be adapted to more precisely reflect upcoming content or address specific student needs; and
- pause for any other reason that helps the teacher better understand the principles and practices associated with the IA.

This process builds a shared and comprehensive understanding of the demonstrated IA. It also allows the mentor to be responsive to the specific needs of the teacher's classroom, readying the teacher to implement the IA with their students.

In some cases, this is where the demonstration ends, with a plan for implementation and the mentor scheduled to observe and collect data (see Chapter 3), and potentially step in (see Chapter 10), in the near future. In other cases, a teacher may want or need a practice opportunity before implementing the IA with their students. In that case, demonstrations are followed by a rehearsal.

IMPLEMENTING REHEARSALS TO SUPPORT TEACHERS' INDEPENDENT PRACTICE

In a demonstration, the mentor is the one who provides the instructional modeling, while either mentor or teacher pauses for discussion. In a rehearsal, the responsibility for modeling is reversed, though both mentors and teachers can ask to pause for problem solving and discussion.

In a *rehearsal*, the teacher uses the same language, materials, body positioning, gestures, and so forth that they intend to use with students in order to "practice" an IA in part or in whole. Rehearsals are *not* talking through or describing what *might* be said and done. They are a "dry run" of what the teacher will actually do with their students. Rehearsals are just as concrete as a mentor's demonstration. This is important. Sometimes an idea seems crystal clear in one's head, but when articulated, the clarity is just not there and that leads to missed opportunities for student learning. For rehearsals to fully support successful application in the classroom, precision counts.

A rehearsal can follow a demonstration or can be implemented on its own as a way for the teacher to practice with the support of a mentor before attempting classroom implementation. At any point during the rehearsal, the teacher or mentor can call a "time out." Some common interactions during rehearsal pauses include (see Gardiner, 2019)

- the mentor recommending or demonstrating a strategy or technique;
- the mentor interjecting with a common student misconception;
- the mentor offering verbal or nonverbal validation, suggestions, or feedback;
- the teacher asking questions or seeking clarification;
- the teacher seeking guidance on potential student-, classroom-, or school-specific concerns;
- working through idea;
- talking through ideas or a sequence of steps;
- problem solving or problem posing;
- correcting misconceptions or mistakes as needed; and
- providing student-friendly examples or more robust academic language.

Rehearsals provide practice opportunities for the teacher in a reduced-complexity setting (i.e., students are not present) where feedback is provided and problem solving can occur. The teacher can then re-rehearse, immediately applying the feedback and adapting the IA to better meet their students' needs. Rehearsing increases the likelihood that subsequent implementation *with* students will be more effective. In addition, rehearsals help teachers see themselves as capable and ready, with the skills, knowledge, and ability to successfully enact the IA being practiced (Gardiner, 2019).

TIPS FOR MAKING REHEARSALS MORE EFFECTIVE

First, if teachers have not experienced rehearsals, mentors may need to provide some context and guidance to ensure rehearsals improve teaching and learning. For example, it is important to establish that the purpose of rehearsals is to increase knowledge, skill, and confidence so that when teachers are with students, they capably deliver ambitious and responsive instruction. Some teachers initially find rehearsals uncomfortable. After all, rehearsals can reveal teachers' misconceptions and gaps in planning, and importantly, illuminate opportunities for improvement.

Some teachers will state that it is easier, and preferable, for them to talk through ideas or just try things with their students and then reflect later. While experience and reflection can certainly facilitate learning, when it comes to teaching, that delay in learning can be at the expense of students. As with any practice, trust and clear discussions of the purpose of the mentoring practice (i.e., "a safe space to try something out with support") are important.

Second, it is also important to situate rehearsals as a practice opportunity that is meant to *inform* teaching, but not constrain it. When a teacher rehearses in the manner described above and receives feedback, they have thought through and practiced the component parts of an IA. They have a game plan for implementation. This prepares them to more fully attend to the complexities of classroom life without having to think through the next steps in their teaching.

However, a rehearsal is not a script. Teachers need to know that when teaching their students, based on their judgment, they may end up using different words or examples, or drawing on teachable moments. While experienced teachers will likely know this, new teachers may benefit from a reminder.

DEMONSTRATIONS AND/OR REHEARSALS IN TANDEM WITH OTHER PRACTICES

Whether used separately or together, after demonstrations and/or rehearsals the teacher and mentor plan for the teacher's subsequent, independent, classroom-based application. This plan includes having the pair select from the full range of mentoring practices to provide ongoing support. Maybe the teacher has the mentor *observe* the IA in practice and collect data (see Chapter 3). Perhaps the mentor will also be prepared to step in (see Chapter 10) and/or video the lesson (see Chapter 7). If the teacher and/or mentor think more highly scaffolded support is needed, the pair may decide to co-plan (see Chapter 6), schedule a collegial visit (see Chapter 8), demonstration teach (see Chapter 11), or co-teach (see Chapter 12).

FINAL THOUGHTS ON DEMONSTRATIONS AND REHEARSALS

Too often teachers leave a debriefing session thinking they are ready for classroom application only to find out that there are gaps in their knowledge or skills that make for uneven teaching and learning experiences. Importantly, when teachers struggle to implement an ambitious IA, there is a tendency to abandon that practice. Demonstrations and rehearsals, used separately or in tandem, can fill an important role in building teachers' capacity and confidence. As part of the debriefing process, both methods help teachers bridge the ideas discussed into their actual classroom teaching.

Demonstrations provide concrete representations that can be paused mid-model for questions, clarifications, and repetition. Rehearsals provide teachers with the opportunity to do a "dry run," again with pauses for feedback and support. Regularly incorporating demonstrations and rehearsals into the debrief can proactively aid teachers to skillfully implement ambitious instruction with all students.

QUESTIONS FOR REFLECTION AND ACTION

1. Have you engaged in demonstrations and/or rehearsals previously? What was the impact? What from the chapter might help you expand the way you conduct these practices (separately or in tandem) with teachers?
2. If you have not engaged in demonstrations and/or rehearsals, how might the information from this chapter inform the way you approach and engage in these practices (separately or in tandem)?
3. Is there anything about these practices that is exciting? That makes you uncomfortable?
4. Consider some of the instructional activities your teachers may need support with (e.g., facilitating discussions, inquiry-based science, analyzing historical documents, analyzing student work). Select one and consider what it might be like to demonstrate or rehearse this IA. How would you frame the experience? What are the key components, and what is their importance? How might that experience unfold?

5. It is quite likely that some teachers will want to talk through, rather than "rehearse," their lesson. How might you respond in that moment to either establish what a rehearsal looks like and its purpose in advance or pause a teacher and have them rehearse rather than describe?

6. Teacher agency is a critical part of both demonstrations and rehearsals. How can you help teachers be more active in the way they pause for problem solving, clarification, and so forth? How can you help teachers initiate demonstrations and rehearsals on their own when they recognize they need the additional support?

Chapter Ten

Stepping Into the Action to Provide "Real-Time" Support

So much is happening in a classroom, and new teachers don't always know how to respond or select from a range of strategies. So stepping in lets them see the effect on students.—Jamila, new teacher mentor

I think the trick is that stepping in has to be positive and acknowledge my teacher's competence, particularly when it's something the students also see. When I step in, I find myself saying sometimes, "Is that right Ms. Hayes?" or something like that.—Sharveta, fifth-year mentor

Everyone who has taught knows that classroom life is complex! In any given day, teachers make more than 1,000 decisions (Jackson, 1990). Teachers who are new to the profession as well as those with more experience can, at times, benefit from in-the-moment support while teaching. This is particularly true when teachers are implementing new instructional activities (IAs), when they have changed grade levels, when they are teaching new content areas, and/or when they are challenged in building or sustaining equitable and productive classroom environments. Stepping in is an inside practice that can be implemented in a range of ways to provide this responsive support.

When mentors *step in*, they interject during instruction to provide cues, impromptu modeling, feedback, and/or engage in quick problem solving that is related to the teacher's goal. By doing so, the mentor is able to capitalize upon the potential of in-the-moment, contextualized learning for teachers and students. Stepping in enhances teaching and learning right then and there, rather than waiting to pose the recommendation in a later debrief.

The broader aim of stepping in, from an educative stance, is helping a teacher achieve their instructional goals. Stepping in, and really any mentoring practice, should be thought of as temporary scaffolding. In this case, the support looks like a mentor stepping into a lesson to provide a model of practice, a cue, or a recommendation, or to co-think. Then, the mentor and teacher follow-up, typically during a debrief, to discuss the insights gleaned and how those insights can later be integrated into the teacher's repertoire or knowledge base. At that point, what was learned via stepping in becomes the teacher's background knowledge, ready to be applied in future teaching.

IMPROMPTU AND PLANNED STEPPING IN

Stepping in can be impromptu, happening in response to what is unfolding in "real time" in the teacher's classroom, or planned in advance. Either way, stepping in provides immediate, in-context support that can improve instruction or help a teacher process and make decisions. Afterward, the mentor and teacher follow up, most often during the debrief, to discuss the impact on the teacher's and students' learning.

Impromptu stepping in might occur while a mentor is collecting data on a predetermined focus. While collecting data, the mentor observes that a few students are confused. The mentor may decide in that moment to step in by raising their hand to ask a clarifying question or writing a quick note and handing it to the teacher. In another case, a mentor may think the teacher could provide a different example that would add more depth to students' learning. Then, they might whisper the idea in the teacher's ear or stand up and interject with a quick example.

Planned stepping in generally begins during a debriefing session when teachers and mentors are talking about next steps for implementing or improving implementation of an IA. Perhaps the teacher would like their mentor to be available as "backup." Or the mentor may believe additional and nuanced support through stepping in would be beneficial based on their previous experiences with the teacher, the students, or the IA.

Whether or not teachers and mentors plan for stepping in, it usually happens in combination with other mentoring practices. For example, in planned stepping in, a teacher who is transitioning to inquiry science from textbook-based instruction might ask a mentor to capture video of their instruction *and* be prepared to provide backup assistance to clarify directions or procedures, or help ensure students are safely, productively, and collaboratively using materials.

In impromptu stepping in, the teacher may have asked the mentor to capture video. However, while capturing video, the mentor notices that the teacher is not providing sufficient wait time between asking a question and seeking student responses. In that moment, the mentor may provide a cue such as holding up a white board that says "wait time" as a reminder.

WAYS TO STEP IN

Educative mentoring is teacher centered and responsive. Mentors, therefore, need to have a range of options for *how* they step in in order to help the teacher meet ambitious learning goals. These can include the following:

- using predetermined and/or clear and simple gestures and nonverbal cues that can help a teacher remember and implement (or provide positive reinforcement for implementing!) a previously discussed practice;
- whispering or passing a brief note to the teacher offering a way to clarify or deepen instruction;
- interjecting during instruction to provide an alternative/additional example that may be more robust or relevant, and so forth;
- holding up a brief message on a white board as a quick reminder, building from a prior discussion;
- quickly interjecting an idea during instruction to elaborate upon, redirect, or enhance the effectiveness of an instructional practice (e.g., if a teacher is working on orienting students to each other's thinking, a mentor might interject and ask, "Jeremy, can you build off of Allina's idea?");
- raising a hand to ask a question that may draw attention to student confusion;
- approaching the teacher with an offer to assist (e.g., "Would you like me to . . . ?" or "How can I help you . . . ?");
- intervening with a student or small group of students to clarify processes, redirect behavior, and/or support learning;
- briefly assuming instructional responsibility and releasing it back to the teacher; and
- modeling an instructional strategy or the use of specific language.

As these examples show, stepping in can be subtle or more overt. Some teachers may be comfortable with any and all stepping in, while others may find more overt ways disruptive. If that is the case, it does not mean a mentor should avoid these forms entirely. Rather, mentors should continue to build relationships with their teacher and the students, and actively use other methods of stepping in.

A final consideration related to stepping in, and really all inside practices, stems from norms in American public education related to individuality, autonomy, authority, and the notion that "great teachers are born not made" (Britzman, 2003; City et al., 2009). Some teachers, therefore, might see their mentor stepping in as a sign of their "failure." These same norms may mean that some mentors think stepping in is only needed if their teacher "is in trouble" or that stepping in is a "crutch" and teachers should learn by doing and reflecting instead. However, to hold to these beliefs is to ignore a robust and highly impactful set of practices that can accelerate and differentiate teacher and student learning.

TIPS FOR MAKING STEPPING IN MORE EFFECTIVE

Regardless of whether stepping in is impromptu or planned, overt or subtle, it is important that mentors and teachers discuss beforehand the purpose for and different possible ways of stepping in. Proactively discussing what stepping in looks like and when it might happen increases the likelihood that stepping in will enhance teacher learning. It also lessens the likelihood that teachers will be thrown off track or that teachers will feel as though their authority is usurped when a mentor steps in.

This important conversation can also increase buy-in and give the teacher a say in the process, determining which stepping-in approach they feel most comfortable with. For example, a mentor could say something like the following:

> I know we've been working on asking more rigorous questions and orienting students to each other's ideas. Here is something I could try. Let me know what you think about it. If there comes a point when I think your practice and student learning could be supported right in the moment, I could give you some signals from the back of the room. I could use short signals on a white board, gestures, or whisper in your ear. Which of these sounds best to you?

In this scenario, the mentor is offering options and working to keep stepping in very subtle, to the point where students will be unlikely to notice the interaction. Also, this conversation ensures that the cues are clear, concise, and focused on the teacher's goal. Together, mentors and teachers decide upon preferred methods of stepping in, while keeping the door open for additional stepping-in methods.

STEPPING IN AND DEBRIEFING SESSIONS

Stepping in is a practice for fostering teachers' professional growth. While some of the learning happens *as stepping in occurs* in the classroom, a great deal of growth happens during the next debriefing session. After stepping in, mentors should facilitate a two-pronged discussion. One prong relates to *understanding how the teacher experienced stepping in*, essentially assessing their comfort. The other relates to *building teachers' knowledge from the experience*.

Assessing teachers' comfort is important because if stepping in is to be an available practice, there needs to be teacher buy-in. Even if teachers are uncertain, conversations to ascertain comfort can be a launching point from which extremely subtle stepping in can open space for more overt stepping in, or even more overt practices like demonstration teaching "inside" (see Chapter 11) and co-teaching (see Chapter 12).

To gauge and respond to teachers' comfort levels, mentors can ask, "How did stepping in work for you when I . . . ?" This question is intended to understand whether the experience worked for the teacher, and for the mentor and teacher to consider the impact on students:

- Did stepping in have a positive impact on students' learning?
- Did stepping in feel relatively seamless, or did students find it distracting in ways that make it hard to reorient to the teacher or the activity they were engaged in?
- What should the mentor do similarly or differently in the future?

As the relationship between mentor and teacher builds, less time will need to be dedicated to assessing comfort, though it is always beneficial for mentors to make space for this conversation.

To prompt learning, mentors can ask the following:

"When I [describe the moment of stepping in], what did you notice/ learn?"

"What can you take away from this experience to inform future teaching [or planning]?"

"What do you think was the impact on students and their learning? What should I/we do similarly/differently in the future?"

Questions such as these help teachers learn from the experience and consider how they will use insights in their future teaching. Such questions also open up space for mentors and teachers to discuss less visible, more nuanced aspects of ambitious teaching and learning. Based on how this discussion unfolds, mentors and teachers determine what other inside and/or outside practices are logical next steps to help teachers further develop their knowledge and skill.

FINAL THOUGHTS ON STEPPING IN

Stepping in provides in-the-moment support to help teachers implement ambitious and equitable instruction. When teachers know a mentor is ready and willing to intercede in a lesson, they may be willing to take more instructional risks. Mentors step in and implement other inside practices, such as demonstration (see Chapter 11) and co-teaching (see Chapter 12), because they believe significant learning for teachers *and* students can result from a mentor's thoughtful guidance as instruction is taking place. Follow-up conversations deepen learning and can open avenues for mentors to continue and expand the range of ways they step in.

Successful stepping in also builds the trust needed for mentors to demonstrate and co-teach. If teachers see that mentors' active engagement with and in their classroom is beneficial, they may be more willing to share greater amounts of instructional time and even turn over instruction to mentors. In this way, stepping in is an important practice in its own right and can set a foundation for other inside practices.

QUESTIONS FOR REFLECTION AND ACTION

1. Have you ever stepped in when a teacher was teaching? In what ways? More subtle? Overt? What went well? What were the challenges?

2. Have you ever had someone step in when you were teaching? What went well? What were the challenges? Did it affect your teaching? If so, how? If not, why not?

3. If stepping in is not currently a regular part of your repertoire, think of the teachers you are working with. Pick one (or more) to focus on. What types of stepping in might be more comfortable or needed? How might you introduce the idea? What would follow-up look like?

4. If stepping in is a regular part of your repertoire, how might the ideas in this chapter help you expand your repertoire or deepen your use of this practice?

5. Stepping in requires buy-in from teachers. How might you (over time) build that buy-in for stepping in when a teacher prefers that their mentor is more of an invisible presence in the classroom?

6. Imagine that after stepping in a teacher started to withdraw from you or appeared to be offended. What would you say? Do? How would you repair the relationship? How might you keep the door open for stepping in in the future?

Chapter Eleven

Demonstration Teaching

Contextualized Mentor Modeling

When you demonstration teach, your teachers can sometimes see that there is a lot more that they and their students are capable of, and . . . hopefully be inspired to up their game.—Kassie, instructional coach

We set the goal of implementing guided reading. My mentor modeled lessons for me with my students. It blew my mind. I may think I know what it looks and sounds like, but when she modeled the lesson in my classroom, I really absorbed it. Then we co-planned and watched videos of her teaching guided reading together. It really helped me put the pieces together.—Monique, first-year teacher

A critical goal of educative mentoring is helping teachers implement ambitious instructional activities (IA) that foster learning for all students. Even when teachers have learned about or observed an IA in action, such as incorporating student-led literature discussions or facilitating historical document analysis, translating these IAs into effective classroom practice can be challenging. It is even more daunting if a teacher has read or heard about an IA, wants to try it, but is unsure exactly what it looks like in action. Demonstration teaching, as an inside practice, lets teachers see an IA in practice with their students.

Demonstration teaching is when a mentor assumes full responsibility for teaching a lesson, part of a lesson, or an instructional routine or procedure to the teacher's class. When mentors demonstration teach, they can illuminate a teacher's instructional goal by making that goal, be it building models to represent mathematical thinking, comparing and contrasting multiple methods to solve real-world mathematics problems, or other complex IAs, concrete *and* contextualized *with the teacher's* students.

While modeling strong practice (i.e., the demonstration) is important, it is only one piece of a broader picture that includes

- sharing lesson plans and making planning clear;
- developing content and pedagogical knowledge as needed;
- determining the teacher's role during the demonstration;
- debriefing to facilitate meaning-making and a change in practice;
- ensuring relationships with teachers and students are strong; and
- ensuring teacher buy-in is strong for the IA.

Each piece needs to be addressed in order for demonstrations to foster teacher development and their ability to skillfully implement the IA reflective of their goal.

BENEFITS OF DEMONSTRATION TEACHING

There are many advantages associated with mentors' demonstration teaching (Gardiner & Weisling, 2016):

- Teachers see complex IAs implemented with their own students, and in some cases, this increases teachers' expectations for what their students are capable of doing.
- Mentors are able to demonstrate their own skills and abilities, potentially building credibility and teacher buy-in for mentorship.
- Teachers can follow up with their mentor to ask questions and problem-solve, thereby deepening their understanding of the IA (unlike when watching an exemplar video).
- Risk and responsibility for trying complex IAs is shared between teacher and mentor.

The combination of these benefits makes demonstration teaching particularly impactful when it comes to accelerating teachers' ability to implement the IAs associated with their goals.

SETTING THE STAGE FOR EFFECTIVE DEMONSTRATION TEACHING

Demonstration teaching is an impactful and complex practice. Its success hinges on a myriad of factors. Mentors should consider the following to help them think through the process of preparing for, enacting, and following up after demonstration teaching.

How Will Lesson Planning Occur?

Demonstration teaching has the mentor taking lead on instruction. Therefore, in order for teachers to eventually take responsibility for implementing the IA, it is vital that the mentor's planning and preparation is transparent. There are options for making this process visible to teachers: co-planning or the mentor could plan alone and then share the plan.

To begin, the *mentor and teacher can co-plan* (see Chapter 6). This can deepen the teacher's conceptual knowledge of the IA as well as how to effectively translate that knowledge into their own planning and instruction. Co-planning also engages the teacher as an active problem solver and draws upon their expertise related to content and students. However, co-planning can be a time-intensive process that may not always be possible.

Alternatively, the *mentor plans alone and then shares and discusses the plan* with the teacher prior to the demonstration. Talking through the plan provides an important preview. It builds teachers' background knowledge for what will happen so they can focus on the instruction as it unfolds, rather than anticipating what might happen next.

This choice can also make sense if the teacher is less experienced with the content or grade level. In this case, the teacher might benefit more from hearing how the mentor made planning decisions, such as how to make the content accessible and rigorous, how to motivate and engage students intellectually, and the routines and procedures that lead to effective teaching and learning.

What Is the Teacher's Role During the Demonstration Lesson?

Teachers need to have an active role in demonstration teaching to make the event meaningful and conducive to transfer. This can happen in different ways:

- Teacher sits with the class or a group of students to support learning and engagement
- Teacher sits separate from students and has an observational focus, taking notes or collecting data (see Chapter 3) to analyze and discuss in the follow-up debriefing session
- Combination of the above

How Will the Experience Be Debriefed to Ensure the Teacher Learns the Deeper Elements That Make the IA Effective?

Debriefing the demonstration increases the likelihood that the teacher gains the insights and knowledge needed to implement the IA independently. Debriefs of demonstration teaching should use the familiar structure shared in Chapter 4:

> What was effective [related to the focus] and why?
>
> What were the challenges [related to the focus] and why?
>
> To making meaningful change in [teacher's] practice, what are the next steps for the teacher? For the mentor?

Teachers' observations, including any data collected, as well as questions derived from the demonstration lesson should play a central role in the debrief. As mentors listen and respond to teachers' insights and queries, they should also keep in mind how they can draw upon the shared experience and any data collected to unpack the nuances that contribute to effective IA implementation.

Ambitious IAs have many moving pieces and require many in-the-moment decisions. When mentors help teachers identify the nuances and see how those pieces work together with their group of students, teachers will be better positioned to successfully take up the IA on their own. For example, if a mentor was facilitating a whole-class discussion, they may want to draw the teacher's attention to their use of wait time, how they asked follow-up questions, or how they re-voiced students' ideas to clarify and uplift important contributions that might have otherwise been missed.

Mentors and teachers may also find it beneficial to record the demonstrated lesson, using the video as a shared point of reference and review. That video can also become a potential exemplar video for future usage (see Chapter 7).

What Is the Plan for the Teacher to Apply What They Learned Through the Demonstration?

This is a critical piece. It is not enough for the teacher to see and discuss the demonstrated IA. After the demonstration, there needs to be a clear and scaffolded path to independent implementation. That path may entail co-teaching (see Chapter 12), co-planning (see Chapter 6), demonstrations and rehearsals (see Chapter 9), or the teacher taking up the IA with the mentor gathering observational data (see Chapter 3) or collecting video (see Chapter 7) and potentially stepping in (see Chapter 10). There are many options to choose from, but a clear path forward that works for the teacher and mentor is essential.

PROACTIVELY ADDRESSING POTENTIAL CONCERNS

While there are clear benefits to demonstration teaching, mentors also share some common concerns when thinking about demonstration teaching (Gardiner & Weisling, 2016). At times, these concerns may prevent mentors from opting to demonstration teach. In some cases, it may *not* be the right practice at a particular time.

Still, demonstrations should be an active part of a mentor's repertoire. The following questions can help mentors think through and proactively respond to these common, and real, concerns while also deciding whether the timing is right to demonstration teach:

What Happens If the Lesson Does Not Go Well?

Even the most skilled educators have lessons that do not go as hoped. Mentors may worry about what a potentially "failed" lesson can do to their credibility. This is where relationships come into play (see Chapter 2). If relationships with students are well developed and the mentor knows students' names, their strengths and needs, and the overall rhythm and routines of the classroom, it is more likely that the lesson will be successful. Strong relationships with their teachers will also likely buy them additional grace and understanding.

Even with relationships and a well-designed plan, a lesson just may not unfold as intended. Mentors who regularly demonstration teach are still able to make the experience meaningful. They begin by being honest in their assessment and making visible the way they reflect upon their teaching, and articulating what they would do differently, why, and how.

In short, mentors consider an "unsuccessful" lesson an opportunity to model the habit of being a reflective practitioner, rather than worry they will lose credibility with their teacher. By modeling honesty and rigorous analysis, mentors find that their relationships with teachers are actually strengthened.

What Happens If the Lesson Goes Too Well?

Mentors sometimes worry about looking like an expert and distancing themselves from their teachers who may think, "I could never do that!" It comes back to relationships, as well as modeling humility and noting the intentional and learnable work that went into the lesson's success.

Mentors can talk about the intentional steps in planning and their in-the-moment decision-making. They can talk about earlier lessons that did not go as well (and why). If they sense their teacher is feeling discouraged by the mentor's success, this may guide their next steps to include more intentional scaffolding such as co-planning (see Chapter 6), demonstrations and/or re-hearsals (see Chapter 9), and/or co-teaching (see Chapter 12).

What If Teachers Just Treat It Like a Break?

This is why it is so important to think through the questions posed in "Setting the Stage for Effective Demonstration Teaching." If teachers are committed to taking up the IA the mentor is going to demonstrate, they are more likely to be invested in learning from the event. Talking through the plan or co-planning helps foreground what will happen, leaving teachers with more attentional resources to observe productively. Also, the experience will be more purposeful and beneficial for teachers if they take an active role during the observation.

What If the IA Is Beyond My Knowledge or Skill Base as a Mentor?

Given that education is constantly evolving, this is a real possibility. This can also be an opportunity for mentors to model humility, problem-solving skills, and continuous professional growth. Based on any number of reasons, some IAs may simply not have been part of their knowledge base or repertoire.

Once again, honest communication and relationships count! Perhaps the mentor explains that this is the first time they will be facilitating this IA. The mentor could position the teacher as the expert and/or co-learner. The subsequent discussion could be fruitful for both mentor and teacher, and the risk-taking could further enhance relationships. Or perhaps the mentor does not currently have time or capacity for this type of time investment. They could suggest co-teaching (see Chapter 12), collegial visits (see Chapter 8), or watching and analyzing a video together (see Chapter 7).

Should I Demonstration Teach This IA With This Teacher at This Time?

When mentors are thinking about offering or agreeing to demonstration teach, here are some quick questions to consider:

- Is the IA one that the teacher is truly motivated to learn? Is it connected to the teacher's professional goals?
- Is there a clear path forward that will lead to independent practice? If so, what other inside/outside practices will be integrated into that path?
- Are my relationships established with teachers and students?
- Can I be a reasonably strong model?

If the answer to any of these questions is no, the timing may not be right for demonstration teaching at this moment. Mentors should consider what other inside/outside practices are a better fit. At the same time, mentors should seek to address factors that prevented demonstration teaching so it can be an option in the future.

FINAL THOUGHTS ON DEMONSTRATION TEACHING

Demonstration teaching is a particularly complex mentoring practice. Effective demonstrations are built upon mentors' strong relationships with teachers and students; mentors' content, grade level, and pedagogic expertise; and the teacher's commitment to taking up a particular IA. On top of all of this, effective demonstrations must include each of the following:

- co-planning (or sharing lesson plans),
- the actual demonstration and deciding how the teacher will be engaged, and
- a debrief that makes meaning of the experience and charts a course forward.

While these factors make demonstration teaching complex, it is also important to recognize the incredible potential demonstrations can hold. Demonstrations can help a teacher see *their goal* enacted with *their students*. Demonstrations can help teachers "see" their students differently, even leading to increased expectations for what students can accomplish.

Demonstrations can show that the mentor is committed, is credible, and has "skin in the game"—all of which strengthen relationships. Even if a demonstration does not go as well as hoped, it is an opportunity for mentors to model both humility and what it means to be a reflective practitioner. Demonstration teaching can also help mentors continue to grow as educators. All of these benefits make demonstration teaching an important part of a responsive mentor's repertoire.

QUESTIONS FOR REFLECTION AND ACTION

1. Have you ever demonstration taught? What went well? What were the challenges?
2. When you consider demonstration teaching, what is your initial reaction? Are there things that you find exciting about this practice? Things that make you uncertain or uncomfortable?
3. If demonstration teaching is or has been in your repertoire, are there any insights from this chapter that could help you augment or fine-tune what you are already doing?

4. Some mentors think that demonstration teaching is too much of a "crutch" or is doing "the heavy lifting" for teachers. How would you respond to this?
5. Think about the teachers you work with currently.

      a. Which one might be most amenable to or benefit from demonstration teaching? How might you approach this teacher? What would you want the teacher's role to be for planning and during instruction?

      b. What might you do if a teacher asks you to demonstrate an IA that you have not previously implemented or know much about?

Chapter Twelve

Co-Teaching

Sharing the Risk and Responsibility for
Ambitious Teaching

While working with a middle school math teacher, she wanted to establish small groups but also tells me she is afraid of letting go of a little control. I knew it would help her try something new and take a risk if we were in it together. So, I offered to co-teach those groups with her. We co-planned and got on the same page for what they'd do in groups, how we'd both circulate and monitor to help them through the process that they're using in their groups, and what I wanted her to pay attention to and get out of the experience. Then afterward, we debriefed what happened. It actually involved a little more time and work than other [mentoring] practices, but it got her to where she wanted to be.—Sharveta, second-year mentor

For most teachers, there comes a time when they want to try a new or particularly complex instructional activity (IA) that they understand fairly well, but they lack full confidence in their abilities to implement it. Or perhaps a teacher is seeking additional support in implementing a previously attempted IA that did not go as well as hoped. In either scenario, demonstration teaching by a mentor would likely offer too much support, while co-planning, video analysis, or stepping in would not likely provide enough. For these situations, *co-teaching*, where teacher and mentor share *equal responsibility* for both planning and instruction, will likely provide just the right degree of support to help teachers take up ambitious IAs.

BENEFITS OF CO-TEACHING

Effective co-teaching occurs within a mentoring cycle. It is preceded by thorough co-planning. Then, the mentor and teacher share the responsibility for implementing the IA with the teachers' students. Afterward, the experience is debriefed, ending with a plan for what the teacher and mentor will do next to deepen and refine the teacher's implementation of the IA. This full sequence makes co-teaching a highly scaffolded and contextualized form of mentoring.

The advantages of co-teaching are essentially the same as demonstration teaching: shared risk, teachers are able to see complex IAs with their own students that can lead to increased expectations, and opportunities to debrief and problem-solve. However, in demonstration teaching, mentors must be reasonably sure they are a strong model as they bear the majority of the risk for implementation of the IA.

Co-teaching, on the other hand, offers more risk distribution. If, for example, neither the mentor nor the teacher is facile with the IA, they could decide to co-teach and try it out together. Or if a teacher has consistently struggled with an IA, co-teaching might lighten the teacher's cognitive or work load enough that they are willing to continue trying and are better able to learn in and from the experience.

If the conditions are right to co-teach, it can also be a powerful way for mentors to build relationships with teachers and show investment in the teacher's improvement (i.e., they are willing to "put some skin in the game" with their teachers), all while accelerating teacher learning. Co-teaching also provides unique opportunities for the mentor to learn about, establish, and/or expand their relationships with their teacher's students. This increased knowledge of and deepened relationships with students can further increase both mentor and teacher readiness for continuing to use inside practices. Co-teaching can also help mentors expand their instructional repertoire without undertaking full classroom responsibility.

SETTING THE STAGE FOR EFFECTIVE CO-TEACHING

First, mentors and teachers have to decide that co-teaching is the best practice at this particular time. Mentors and teachers make this decision during the "next steps" portion of a debrief. When determining if co-teaching is the right practice, mentors should ask themselves the following:

"Is co-teaching related to a goal the teacher is committed to?"
"Is sharing full responsibility for planning and facilitating the lesson the most appropriate level of scaffolding for this teacher?"

"Does the mentor have a positive relationship with the teacher and students?"

Like demonstration teaching, co-teaching is a complex practice that encompasses planning, teaching, and a debrief. Unlike demonstration teaching, where the mentor could plan alone or co-plan with the teacher, co-planning is an integral part of co-teaching. When co-planning, there are two main pieces that need attention: (1) a *thorough* plan for instruction that includes the content and pedagogies needed for rigorous and responsive learning (i.e., what to teach, how, and why); and (2) the roles and responsibilities the mentor and teacher will take during instruction (i.e., the co-teaching model).

When it comes to co-teaching, clarity counts! Nothing should be left ambiguous. Mentor and teacher need a shared vision for how the lesson will unfold. Both mentor and teacher must know what they will be doing, or not doing, at each point of the lesson. Both need to understand to what extent and which types of interjections (i.e., verbal, nonverbal, etc.) are welcome, and if so, what they will look and sound like. During co-planning the mentor or teacher can also note areas of concern so that the other can be prepared to step in and provide support as needed.

There are many ways mentors and teachers can allocate their work. Often when mentors and teachers co-teach, they have chosen this practice because the IA they are working on is complex, with many important component parts that relate to content, pedagogy, and student thinking and learning. Without this deliberate attention to content, pedagogy, roles, and responsibilities as part of the co-planning process, co-teaching can turn into a chaotic and frustrating experience.

To guide decisions about roles and responsibilities, models of co-teaching taken from partnerships between general and special educators can be used. The most commonly used and recommended models, adapted for mentoring partnerships from Friend and Cook (2016), are as follows:

- *Team teaching.* Both teacher and mentor are *equally* responsible for planning and participate *equally* in the delivery of instruction to all students; there is no "lead" teacher. This model requires significant trust and the most detailed planning.
- *One teach/one support.* One person takes lead on instruction while the other supports with managing materials, supporting a positive learning climate, trouble-shooting (e.g., if technology is being used), working with one or a small group of students, collecting targeted data, and generally being "on call" to step in and support. *Either* mentor or teacher can play either role, and the pair may choose to alternate throughout the lesson.

In both of these models, the mentor and teacher interact with intentionality and the mentor and teacher can see each other in action throughout the lesson.

There are three other models that mentors and teachers might use. All three distribute responsibility for instruction between mentor and teacher by dividing the students into groups that are led by the mentor *or* teacher. While this lowered student-teacher ratio can facilitate risk-taking on the part of the teacher and facilitate relationship building between the mentor and groups of students, it also limits the opportunity for both mentor and teacher to observe and learn from one another's practice. Therefore, during each of these models, mentor, teacher, or both should consider video recording their portion of the teaching for later analysis:

- *Parallel teaching.* Mentor and teacher divide the class equally and teach the same full lesson content simultaneously to different groups of students.
- *Alternative teaching.* Mentor and teacher divide the class and take responsibility for teaching different-sized, differentiated groups.
- *Centers/stations teaching.* Both teacher and mentor lead different stations connected to the same content that students rotate through. Each student encounters each station and facilitator.

Once the model of co-teaching has been selected and the lesson co-planned, it is time to *co-teach.* With such attention paid to planning and roles, the experience should be rewarding to the teacher, mentor, and students. Clearly, nothing goes fully as planned, but such deliberate planning and attention to details can help the mentor and teacher pivot, as needed, based on a shared understanding of the instructional aims.

Ideally, within 24–48 hours of co-teaching, if not that same day, the teacher and mentor will meet to *debrief,* largely following the steps laid out in Chapter 4. The pair should consider which elements went well, which were challenging, and what potential next steps should be taken, all using evidence from the shared experience. Mentors may find that video recording the co-taught lesson/portion of a lesson and using video analysis (see Chapter 7) can strengthen the shared understanding of these considerations. Together the teacher and mentor create a plan to support the teacher toward implementing the instructional activity on their own, which can include demonstrations and/or rehearsals (see Chapter 9), subsequent observations and data collection (see Chapter 3) with the mentor possibly stepping in (see Chapter 10), and more.

PROACTIVELY ADDRESSING POTENTIAL CONCERNS

The most common considerations and concerns mentors voice about co-teaching are essentially the same as with demonstration teaching (see Chapter 11). Their ideas for responding to these are also essentially the same. There can be concerns about the lesson "failing" and the mentor potentially losing credibility in the eyes of the teacher (or students). Relatedly, the mentor (or teacher) may worry that *their portion* of the lesson will be significantly stronger or weaker than their colleague's part. There may also be concerns about a lack of investment on the part of the teacher, treating co-teaching as a break, or that co-teaching provides support in the moment but does not lead to independent practice.

These legitimate concerns can be addressed in the same ways that mentors foster a climate that leads to productive demonstration teaching. First, mentors must build relationships with teachers and students. If trust between *mentor and teacher* and *mentor and students* is strong, it is more likely that the lesson will be successful. Where a lesson is not successful but there is high trust, teachers will be more open to seeing the mentor model being an effective and reflective practitioner.

Mentors must maintain honest communication, which helps both mentors and teachers navigate these potential challenges. Mentors must ensure that teachers are committed to the IA. They must make the time for thorough and collaborative co-planning, so that the teaching will likely unfold in anticipated ways. And if it does not, a shared image of what successful implementation looks like helps mentors and teachers adjust in principled and responsive ways.

A final consideration is that the co-teaching cycle of co-planning, co-teaching, and debriefing can be particularly time consuming for both mentor and teacher. Effective co-teaching requires that mentors have or develop significant context, content, curricular, and pedagogic knowledge. Therefore, before deciding to co-teach, the mentor and teacher should both have a high degree of certainty that the lesson is unlikely to be canceled (e.g., the mentor is pulled for sub coverage or if there are patterns of scheduling inconsistencies). Mentors must also have the requisite capacities and time required to effectively co-teach.

FINAL THOUGHTS ON CO-TEACHING

Co-teaching is a highly supportive mentoring practice. Co-teaching shares the risk and responsibility for implementing ambitious instruction across mentor and teacher. The related co-planning not only facilitates smoother implementation but also can deepen a teacher's understanding of the IA.

Knowledge is further deepened and translated into future action during the debrief.

Co-teaching and demonstration teaching are complex practices that mentors tend to use less often (Gardiner, 2017; Gardiner & Weisling, 2016; Schwille, 2008). However, these practices can accelerate teacher and student learning because they are so comprehensive and contextualized. Given how much time teachers spend in classrooms with students, not using these practices, when the conditions are right to do so, can be a missed opportunity. Mentors should thoughtfully and regularly use (and be encouraged and supported to use) co-teaching in conjunction with other mentoring practices to move teachers toward their professional goals.

QUESTIONS FOR REFLECTION AND ACTION

1. Have you ever co-taught? What went well? What were the challenges? Are there any insights from this chapter that could help you augment or fine-tune what you are already doing?
2. When you consider co-teaching, what is your initial reaction? Are there things that you find exciting about this practice? Things that make you uncertain or uncomfortable?
3. How might the information in this chapter help you weave into/increase the use of co-teaching in your repertoire?
4. Think about the teachers you work with currently. Which one might be most amendable to or benefit from co-teaching? How might you approach this teacher?

Part III

Mentoring the Mentor

Chapter Thirteen

Mentoring the Mentors

Learning to mentor has been such a steep learning curve! Our professional development has been really good. Our directors gave us the theory, and then they really drilled down. So, you could actually see "Here's a [data collection] tool. Here are the conditions for that tool. This is how you would use it. Now you practice. Now, practice again." But perhaps my best learning came from seeing other mentors do mock debriefs and mentor their teachers. It still doesn't really prepare you for some of the variability that happens, but it helps.—Joelle, first-year mentor

Professionals in every stage of their career benefit from purposeful and well-designed professional development (PD), feedback, and ongoing support. Mentors are no exception. Most mentors were once experienced classroom teachers with a demonstrated track record of success. Yet, as this book shows, mentoring requires a separate, specialized knowledge base and skill set that, to be developed, requires time, training, and support.

It may seem obvious that new mentors face a "steep learning curve" as they transition into their new role, and will need high-quality PD and support. Potentially less obvious is that experienced mentors also benefit from opportunities to build upon, deepen, and in some cases, challenge their existing knowledge and practice base.

The final section of this book outlines three effective practices that mentoring programs and individual mentors can draw upon to support mentor development:

1. *Video analysis and self-reflection* (see Chapter 14) provides a visual model for purposeful analysis of a mentoring practice. Independently or collaboratively, mentor(s) can view and analyze their own or exem-

plar videos following a process similar to what was described between mentors and teachers in Chapter 7.

2. *Co-mentoring* (see Chapter 15) is a collaborative, nonevaluative practice in which two or more mentors engage in a process of mutual exploration and improvement of a mentoring practice(s). The co-mentoring process is modeled after the reflective mentoring cycle used with teachers. Even though collaborating mentors may have different levels of experience and expertise, they are learning together.

3. *Mentor development sessions* (MDSs; see Chapter 16) are designed from an educative stance. In an MDS, a program lead, more experienced mentor, or mentor whose practice is beyond their colleague's facilitates the learning of another, less experienced mentor, in a process that parallels the mentor-teacher mentoring cycles (e.g., goal setting, observations, debriefs, with a range of inside/outside practices strategically selected and utilized within each step). An MDS may or may not be part of a mentor's evaluation process.

All three of these mentor-support structures have unique characteristics, and each can affect mentors' practice in distinctive ways that are explored in subsequent chapters.

SETTING THE STAGE

These three mentor-the-mentor practices are methods of supporting mentors *after they have begun actively mentoring teachers.* Therefore, before engaging in video analysis, co-mentoring, or MDSs, specific mentoring knowledge and skills must be foregrounded. This foregrounding includes providing initial and ongoing PD, setting goals, and applying a mentoring cycle *for and with* mentors.

Provide Mentor-Specific PD Before and During the School Year

Before critically analyzing their own practices or the practice of other mentors, mentors must first be *exposed to* and *understand* key mentoring concepts such as

- principles of educative mentoring;
- how to effectively engage and support adult learners;
- scaffolding (including responsive, flexible support, and fading) and how it can bring about learning;
- nimbly and effectively using a variety of observational tools and inside/outside practices; and

- establishing, sustaining, and negotiating relationships with teachers, students, and administrators.

Mentors may also need specific opportunities to maintain or expand their knowledge within content areas, grade levels, standards, and pedagogical approaches. Introductions to these concepts are best delivered via intentionally designed, responsive, and engaging PD that occurs *in conjunction with* video, co-mentoring, and MDSs. Suggested topics, timelines, and additional resources for mentor PD can be found in Appendix C.

Design Educative Mentor PD With an Eye Toward Active and Applied Learning

Educative mentoring offers a vision of mentoring as scaffolded, collaborative, situated in teachers' work, and aimed at improving instruction. It is important that mentors deeply understand this vision first and foremost. With that foundation in place, mentors can learn to translate that vision into practice through PD that is designed and facilitated in ways that model the principles of adult learning that mentors are expected to use in their own practice:

- Information is presented in relevant, engaging, and differentiated ways.
- Theory/practice connections are made so mentors can make informed, flexible, teacher-centered decisions.
- Demonstrations are incorporated and modeled by an experienced mentor, providing case studies, reviewing video, and so forth, followed by mentor rehearsals with feedback and time for Q & A.
- Problems of practice are discussed with multiple perspectives emphasized.

PD that is designed with these principles in mind provides mentors with a comprehensive introduction to relevant mentoring concepts and skills, as well as opportunities to reflect and practice with feedback. This, in turn, ensures mentors are ready to flexibly and responsively apply those concepts and skills with the teachers they support. Mentors' implementation can then be supported with feedback provided through one or more mentor-support practices, described below and in the subsequent chapters.

Use Video to Support Learning

When *introducing or deepening knowledge of data collection tools or mentoring practice*, videos are an excellent resource for learning. Exemplar videos show a strong model of practice. Videos can be paused for discussion and analysis, for questions to be raised and discussed, and to highlight critical features. Those leading PD should use pauses during the viewing or time after for mentors to rehearse the practice or apply the data collection tool with feedback and support from one another.

Alternatively, videos can be a launch for applied practice. Imagine a team is being introduced to the seating chart tool (see Chapter 3). After learning about the purpose and ways for using the tool, mentors may view a video of classroom instruction. As they view the video, they practice collecting seating chart data. After they finish the video and review their data, mentors can share and discuss data with each other, noting similarities and any discrepancies. Doing so helps mentors refine their use of the tool before working with teachers.

As discussed earlier, mentors will need to build their knowledge of ambitious IAs. Teaching videos can be an excellent resource. Following the same processes described above, videos can be viewed, paused, and discussed with critical features marked, and rewatched to provide additional clarity and depth of knowledge. The Teaching Channel, the New Teacher Project, High Leverage Practice from the CEEDAR Center, Teaching Works at University of Michigan, and Annenberg Learner all provide videos depicting ambitious instruction. Virtually all are free, but some Teaching Channel and Teaching Works videos have fees.

Procuring exemplar videos of mentoring practices in action can be a challenge. Mentors or leaders of mentoring programs should therefore be proactive in collecting videos from other mentor colleagues. Program leads can also look ahead at what practices will be introduced or that mentors typically struggle with and set about capturing videos of themselves or other veteran mentors enacting these practices.

Embed Mentor Development Flexibly and in Cycles Focused on Goals (Just as Mentors Do With Teachers)

As mentors learn and deepen their knowledge about mentoring—what educative mentoring is, why it is important, and how to flexibly enact an educative practice—they need the same types of professional support given to teachers. Essentially, just as teachers need to identify elements of their teaching practice they want to work on, so do mentors. And just as it is most effective to mentor teachers within inquiry-based cycles (see Chapter 1) that begin with clear goals, the same holds true for mentoring mentors.

Set Initial and Ongoing Goals

Initial goal setting for mentors can be accomplished in a variety of ways. For new mentors, goal setting should occur early in the school year, or even before the year starts. Returning mentors may benefit from setting goals at the start of the school year or at the end of the previous school year. Goals should be based on a range of factors, including self-, peer , and/or supervisor evaluations, as well as programmatic goals and standards. Feedback from teachers and administrators should also be considered.

Mentors' goals, initial and ongoing, often fall into one of the following three areas: deepening existing practices, expanding one's repertoire, or mentoring in a challenging context.

Deepening Existing Practices

All mentors can benefit from goals centered on deepening their knowledge and skill set in *enacting* mentoring practices. For example, new mentors especially may struggle with prioritizing their mentoring focus or identifying the type of data to collect during an observation, and would benefit from a colleague's fresh set of eyes.

Likewise, it is not uncommon for new mentors who are selective scripting to overuse this tool or find themselves scripting *everything* they hear in the classroom rather than focusing on selective segments of language. They may want support in identifying aspects of classroom language to selectively script so that the data they collect are useful when they debrief with teachers (see Chapters 3 and 4 for more exploration).

Mentors across their careers may struggle with aspects of the debriefing sessions such as asking questions that are open-ended yet focused enough to facilitate teachers' reflection on the focal area of their classroom practice. Similarly, new and veteran mentors may want to focus on knowing when to shift between *facilitative language* that supports co-problem solving and reflecting to *instructive language* that builds knowledge by sharing specific ideas and recommendations. Experienced mentors may also simply want to deepen the practices they regularly or comfortably employ.

Expanding One's Repertoire

Many mentors benefit from goals that aim to *expand* their repertoire, supporting them in using mentoring practices or data collection tools that are implemented less frequently but can have great positive impact. When investigating what mentoring practices are used less often, it is typically video analysis, co-teaching, demonstration teaching (both outside and inside), and collegial visits. There are many reasons this might be the case, and mentors may want to look at all the inside and outside practices to self-assess which they use more and less frequently and why. Just as in the way that mentors can share the risk with teachers to try out new instructional activities, mentors can support each other and distribute the risk of trying new practices as well.

Also, mentors tend to find comfort in using certain data collection tools. They have found success in learning how to use them effectively to collect and share data. At times, tools get overused and repertoires need to be expanded.

Mentoring in a Challenging Context

Every mentor will, at some point in their career, need support working with a particular teacher, grade level, or content area. This is not to cast blame on the mentor or teacher but to recognize that teaching as well as fostering and sustaining relationships with teachers is complex. Mentors may, therefore, set goals focused on strengthening interactions with a specific teacher.

For example, a mentor who taught in elementary classrooms may find themselves mentoring a middle school science teacher and want opportunities to observe/be observed by a mentor with a science and/or middle school background. Another mentor may perceive resistance from a teacher who rejects or argues against ideas generated in mentoring conversations, who is not engaging in mentoring conversations, and/or who seemingly does not follow through on next steps. And still another mentor may seek out support in facilitating debriefs that focus on particularly challenging topics such as a teacher's tone of voice or equity of practices with a particular group of students. There are also times when a mentor's intentions and impact do not align, and it may be helpful to have another perspective on how to develop or repair a relationship.

Mentoring Mentors in Flexible, Continuous, and Responsive Cycles

The point here is that mentoring is complex and mentors should feel comfortable acknowledging their challenges and maintaining their own habit of seeking continuous professional growth by setting goals. Then, with their goal in mind, mentors create actionable next steps that are carried out in cycles similar to the mentoring cycles used to support teachers.

To meet their goals, mentors select from the available support structures—video analysis, co-mentoring, and MDSs—integrating them into mentoring cycles in flexible ways based on mentors' preferences, as well as what structures can be put in place given a mentor's context.

MENTORING THE MENTOR: THE AIM

The aim of these final chapters is to outline purposeful, nuanced, and responsive mentor support, foregrounded in principles of educative mentoring. That way, *all* mentors can have what they need to increase their efficacy and, by extension, improve teacher and student learning.

Mentors do this challenging and important work in a wide range of contexts. Some are full-release mentors while others are teaching full time.

Some mentors are the only mentor in the school or district; others work in a team of mentors. Mentors work with teachers in-person or virtually. Mentors might work as content experts or generalists. Mentors may work with preservice or new teachers, or with teachers across career phases from preservice to veteran. The mentor-the-mentor chapters explore the practices of video analysis, co-mentoring, and MDS with full respect for and attention to the many ways mentors engage in their work.

QUESTIONS FOR REFLECTION AND ACTION

1. What was your learning curve like as a new mentor? What did you initially find rewarding? Challenging? Which rewards/challenges did you anticipate? Which surprised you?
2. Review the recommendations for mentor professional development. Which reflect your experiences? Are there any recommendations you would add? Which might you like to see brought into the mentoring program in which you work?
3. In what ways have you used or experienced video as a resource for professional development? Explore some of the teaching videos and resources suggested to see if any might be of use for PD or possibly to share with teachers related to procuring resources: Teaching Channel, High Leverage Practice from the CEEDAR Center, New Teacher Project, Teaching Works at University of Michigan, and Annenberg Learner.
4. How do you grow professionally as a mentor? What support would you find most effective? What support(s) might you contribute to others?

Chapter Fourteen

Video Analysis

A Visual Support for Mentor Growth

I really see the value in reviewing videos of my own practice. It allows me to really see [my practice], you know, with my own eyes and then I find myself thinking, "Oh, I really didn't know I said that" or "I did that so quick—it's only been two minutes?" You can see exactly all the moves you made—or didn't make. It is, for me, really intense. It is like 45 minutes of "Oh, I should have done that" or "that was good." It's kind of like that kind of an eye-opening experience for me and I really want to do more videotaping.—Delilah, first-year mentor

It is not uncommon for professionals to use video to improve their practice. Professional athletes regularly examine video footage of themselves to improve their form, technique, and accuracy. Similarly, actors regularly watch their performances to adjust timing, movements, and projection. As discussed in Chapter 7, teachers who are mentored from an educative stance regularly review videos with their mentor to make improvements to any and all aspects of their professional practice. It should be no surprise then, given the complexities and nuances associated with educative mentoring, that mentors too can benefit from video analysis.

Video analysis is a versatile and highly effective practice that supports mentors' professional growth. Mentoring practices are intricate and require quick, in-the-moment adjustments in order to be responsive. Videos, which can be slowed down, paused, and rewatched, are therefore a valuable option for mentor learning.

While video analysis can be used for capturing any mentoring practice, most mentors tend to use videos to analyze how they facilitate entire debriefing sessions (see Chapter 4). Alternatively, mentors can select and analyze a portion such as "What's Working/What's Challenging?" or practices that typically occur during the "Facilitating Meaningful Change in Practice" portion such as demonstrations and rehearsals (see Chapter 9).

Given that inside practices are especially complex, mentors can benefit from capturing and analyzing videos of when they step in (see Chapter 10), demonstration teach (see Chapter 11), and co-teach (see Chapter 12). Analyzing what went well, areas for improvement, and related next steps can increase mentors' sense of confidence and readiness, as well as support and encourage increased use of typically underused inside practices.

There are three forms of video analysis from which mentors most often choose: video of one's own practice, co-analyzing a peer's video, and an exemplar video. Regardless of the format chosen, to maximize the impact of video analysis, mentors should follow a procedure similar to the one used when analyzing video with their teachers (see Chapter 7). Doing so allows for in-depth analysis and the identification of concrete next steps for professional growth.

SETTING THE STAGE FOR EFFECTIVE VIDEO ANALYSIS

Because there are so many options for engaging in video analysis, to get started mentors must *determine the who, the what, and the how* of the analysis.

Determining the Who: Selecting an Audience for Video Analysis

Once the decision to analyze video has been made, mentors need to determine *who* will review the video and *what* will be reviewed. Mentors may work independently. Or they may choose to work in pairs or small groups based on any number of factors such as grade level, content, specific goals, and similar or mixed levels of expertise (see Chapter 15 for an exploration of potential partnerships).

Before mentors engage in video analysis, either in pairs or small groups, some norms need to be set:

- The video is for the involved mentors' eyes and ears only unless otherwise agreed upon by the mentor being videotaped.
- The purpose of the video is to learn from practice, not to place judgment.
- Conversations that result from viewing the video are confidential.

Regardless of whether a mentor reviews video of themselves, a peer, or an exemplar, the analysis must begin by determining a clear focus.

Determining the What: Choosing a Focus for Video Analysis

To ensure that the video analysis is purposeful and learning is maximized, mentors must begin the process by establishing a *clear focus* for the analysis. This focus should center on facilitating progress toward a mentor's professional goals (see Chapter 13 for more information about goal setting) and/or responding to a more immediate mentor need.

In the case of analyzing video to support mentoring goals, perhaps a mentor has a goal to expand their repertoire of mentoring practices. As part of this goal, they may have opted to co-plan with a teacher for the first time. This mentor may videotape their first co-planning session in order to self-evaluate and/or receive specific feedback from a colleague on what went well and where they can improve. Another mentor may have a goal to co-teach with one or more of their teachers and therefore opt to record their co-taught lessons for analysis.

In the case of responding to an immediate need, a mentor may believe that a teacher's insufficient progress toward a goal is because, as the mentor, they are not communicating effectively enough. For example, a mentor may worry they are doing too much of the talking and thinking during the debrief, thereby denying the teacher sufficient time to ask questions and fully participate in problem solving. This mentor may decide to video a debrief and analyze, or co-analyze, with a clear focus on engaged communication and equity of voice.

As mentioned above, many mentors across their careers choose to use video analysis to improve their *debriefing sessions*. This is no surprise given how critical this portion of the mentoring cycle is. To support this vital practice, some potential foci for analyzing debriefing sessions include but are by no means limited to the following:

- *Clarity of mentoring language.* Is the mentor using language that is free from unfamiliar technical jargon? Are there indications that the teacher is understanding?
- *Teaching versus telling.* Is the mentor modeling effective teaching practices including metacognition and checking for the teacher's understanding? Or is the mentor lecturing without sufficiently engaging the teacher in active knowledge construction?
- *Facilitating meaningful change in teacher's practice.* Is the mentor using demonstrations/rehearsals to their full potential (i.e., pausing for problem solving, using exact language, and so on; see Chapter 9)? Are next steps for the teacher and mentor clear and doable within the timeframes allocated?
- *Equity of voice.* Is the mentor providing enough time for the teacher to think through their ideas, raise questions, and ensure the conversation

reflects the teacher's needs, not just the mentor's agenda? Is the mentor intentionally seeking to increase the teacher's role and responsibility in actively identifying goals, problem solving, and charting their own course forward?

- *Alignment to the mentoring focus.* Is the mentor facilitating goal-aligned analysis and problem solving? When conversations veer, is the mentor able to respectfully attend to what the teacher is saying and needs, while steering the conversation back to the goal? Does the mentor help the teacher "unpack" their goal into logical steps so that the teacher sees, understands, and helps make decisions as to which next step is the most logical and useful?

- *Responding to teacher "pushback" or "excuse making."* Is the mentor using a range of mentoring practices and language to understand, respond to, challenge, and hold teachers accountable for what they say about their practice, their students, and/or the school context?

- *Holding themselves to high standards of equitable practice.* Does the mentor support all teachers responsively and with fairness? Does the mentor ensure that they are looking for and pressing teachers to include and support all learners, particularly those with marginalized identities?

While debriefing is one of the most common video analysis focuses, mentors may also want to examine their implementation of inside practices such as stepping in, co-teaching, and demonstration teaching. Some potential elements of each inside practice mentors may want to review and/or receive feedback on are featured in Table 14.1. These examples, which are by no means an exhaustive list, illustrate that there are many potential foci for nearly any mentoring practices.

Determining the How: Using Data and Debriefing Protocols to Facilitate Professional Growth

Once a focus had been identified, mentors then determine *how* to maximize the potential impact of their video analysis. They must first determine which *type of data to collect* in order to better understand that aspect of practice. These data will then be analyzed and acted upon during a *debriefing* process.

In determining which data to collect, most likely one of the tools used with teachers (see Chapter 3), with minor tweaks, will suffice. For example, if the mentor is reviewing a video of a debrief with a teacher to determine whether equity of voice is present, they may opt to use a two-column selective scripting template to record *their* language as well as the *teachers'*.

Or if they facilitated a rehearsal, they may want to turn the rehearsal structure and possible ways of engaging during pauses into a checklist to ensure they are not inadvertently skipping portions. A checklist can also help

Table 14.1. Guiding questions for analyzing use of inside mentoring practices

Stepping In	Co-teaching	Demonstration Teaching
• Which method of stepping in did I use? Is there another form that may have worked better? • Should I expand the methods I use for stepping in? • How does it appear the stepping in was received by the teacher? The students? • Did my stepping in appear to enhance the learning and/or safety in the classroom? • Was my contribution accurate and effective?	• Did the teacher and I share responsibility for instruction? • Did instruction unfold in a coherent way? • Was the distribution of roles and responsibilities effective for teacher and student learning? If so, why? If not, why not? • What elements of my instruction (content, pedagogy, student engagement) do I want to work on for future demonstrations?	• Was the way I engaged students in the content effective? Why/why not? • What was the teacher's/students' reaction to the demonstration? • What elements of my instruction (content, pedagogy, student engagement) do I want to work on for future co-teaching? • Was the teacher engaged in ways that support their learning, or (as appropriate) student learning?

mentors identify the range of interaction pauses they use. For the latter, the mentor may find they are over- or underusing interaction forms and then use the data and analysis to set a goal to expand their repertoire.

The final step of any video analysis, and the space where most meaningful change to mentor practice happens, is the *debrief*. Based on the data they collected while viewing the selected video, mentors should follow a modified version of the debriefing procedure used with teachers (see Chapter 4).

The first phase of this debriefing experience has mentors posing the questions: "What's working? What did I observe related to the focus that was effective? What made X work/effective? What did I observe in the mentor's practice (mine or a peer) and in the teacher's responses that indicate this is working?" While mentors may be tempted to breeze over this portion of the self- and peer reflection, it is important for mentors to have a balanced perspective and sustain and share aspects of their mentoring practice that are effective.

This should be followed by reflections on new and continuing challenges mentors should consider: "As I reflect on [focus area], what is still challenging? What do I notice about the data related to . . . ? What do I notice about the teacher's response?" In reviewing their own videos, mentors, like their teachers, may be tempted to focus on nonrelevant "challenges" such as how they look and sound. While this is to be expected, mentors should be careful to hone in on areas of growth related to and that will help improve upon their area of focus, using the data, and/or mentoring standards to support their reflections and analysis.

Finally, mentors should ask and answer, "How can I facilitate meaningful change to my/my peer's practice? What are meaningful next steps I/my peer can take to improve? What supports are needed and from where/who?" Now that the mentor has identified areas of growth, they must prioritize and create action steps to facilitate improvement in the focus area, considering which inside/outside practices they might use with teachers as follow-up, or what other PD or support they personally need to help them meet their goals.

Mentors may find they need to procure resources and build more knowledge of an IA, or grade level or content standards. Perhaps they will need to do some readings or attend a conference or professional development to build their knowledge base. Perhaps they will want to be observed by (or observe) a colleague or capture video again.

FACE-TO-FACE AND VIRTUAL REVIEW AND ANALYSIS

When analyzing video with a colleague(s), mentors will need to determine whether face-to-face or virtual review will better meet their needs and constraints. Either works well. It is up to mentors to determine which format or combination of formats will be most useful and doable. Regardless of choice, collaborating mentors will need to

- be clear on the focus for analysis;
- determine which data collection tool to use (selecting the most useful tool can be done in advance of the viewing, or during);
- decide whether to review the video and collect data individually and then come together to discuss and analyze, or complete all steps collaboratively; and
- debrief the experience collaboratively, in person or virtually, using the steps outlined above.

When co-analyzing video virtually, mentors may find applications such as Big Blue Button, Skype, Zoom, FaceTime, and Google Hangouts especially helpful. Virtual platforms are particularly helpful for mentors who work outside a mentoring team or program, or whose school placements make face-to-face viewing difficult.

BENEFITS AND CONSIDERATIONS OF VIDEO ANALYSIS OF SELF AND PEERS

Video allows mentors to *see* their own practice, rather than relying on their memory of events or feedback filtered through another mentor's perspective. Videos also allow mentors to simultaneously hear verbal and see nonverbal interactions with their teachers. It can help them become even more skillful and nuanced in the way they collect and use data as well as with how they grow in their ability to responsively implement a full repertoire of mentoring practices. The subsequent analysis can lead to concrete, actionable next steps for improving mentors' ability to support their teachers and their teachers' students more effectively.

Yet, it is important to recognize that some mentors may feel uncomfortable with viewing videos of themselves, being watched by others, or even viewing and responding to colleagues' videos. Some mentors may feel insecure or embarrassed about seeing their "weaknesses" or making their practice public. Some mentors may struggle to give critical feedback for fear of being "harsh," hurting the other mentor's feelings, or damaging relationships. In particular, some new mentors may be reticent to fully participate in video analysis, believing they lack the experience and expertise to provide useful analysis and feedback.

Norms of collegiality, values of continuous learning, and relational trust are all important steps. Equally important is ensuring confidentiality and that any data collected and discussions held during the debrief are goal aligned. When these factors are in place, new and veteran mentors are more likely to want to engage in video analysis and will experience the many benefits to using video analysis of their own practice.

FINAL THOUGHTS ON VIDEO ANALYSIS AS A TOOL FOR MENTOR GROWTH

Video analysis takes time and can be a vulnerable experience. Yet, just like the great growth potential for teachers when they make their practice public and engage in video analysis, the same holds true for mentors. In addition, mentors can then demonstrate that they practice what they preach and draw upon their own experiences when working with teachers.

Mentors typically have habits of reflective practice and experience facilitating mentoring cycles. As such, a single mentor can gain a great deal of insight that leads to actionable change by viewing and analyzing their own video. At the same time, viewing, analyzing, and problem solving with colleagues provides additional perspectives. These factors make self- and peer video analysis an important practice in the development and ongoing support of educative mentors.

QUESTIONS FOR REFLECTION AND DISCUSSION

1. Have you ever used video analysis of your own practice? What went well? What were the challenges?
2. When you consider video analysis of your own practice, what is your initial reaction? Are there things you find exciting about this practice? Things that make you uncertain or uncomfortable?
3. How might the information in this chapter help you weave video analysis into your repertoire on your own or with peers? Face-to-face or virtually?
4. If video analysis is or has been in your repertoire, are there any insights from this chapter that could help you augment or fine-tune what you are already doing?

Chapter Fifteen

It Takes Two (or More)

Co-Mentoring for Improved Practice

I think that co-mentoring really opens your eyes! It's so helpful to have that other set of eyes where we go in looking at the same focus yet they can pinpoint things that maybe I might have missed, or because there are just so many things going on in the classroom that I focus on certain things and they're maybe focusing on a different aspect that's also important. It's so helpful to see how somebody else sees the situation! Sometimes I'm like, "Oh, I missed that!" And then to hear someone else's suggestions for the teacher! Being able to come together and prioritize, like I saw this and they saw this, and let's see what is the best for the teacher, what can help her improve her instruction the best. I get so many ideas!—Lynda, first-year mentor

Educative mentoring is a lot of things: fast-paced, dynamic, rewarding, challenging, and as has been often stated throughout this book, complex! Like teachers, educative mentors are never "done" when it comes to their learning. Also like the teachers they serve, mentors benefit from a range of flexible and responsive supports that facilitate their professional growth. *Co-mentoring* is an adaptable practice that brings together two or more mentors to engage in a reciprocal, collaborative cycle of examining, analyzing, and improving their mentoring practice.

Co-mentoring partnerships can take many forms. Partnerships can be based on mentoring experience as well as grade level and content expertise. Regardless of the formation, co-mentoring is nonevaluative, meaning there is no hierarchy to the partnership. Co-mentors are peers, engaging in a back-and-forth exchange, moving fluidly between mentoring and being mentored, in a way that leads to mutual learning and growth. Additionally, because mentoring programs come in all configurations, co-mentoring can be in-person or virtual.

ESTABLISHING CO-MENTORING COLLEAGUES

As a mentor-support strategy, co-mentoring looks *between mentors*, rather than to a team leader, supervisor, or evaluator, to identify mutually beneficial learning relationships across colleagues, allowing mentors to learn from and alongside one another. There are multiple possible configurations for mentor teams, and different choices may serve different purposes.

Because all mentors bring different strengths and needs to the table, and because early career mentors often lack the professional acumen and nuance of their veteran counterparts, programs should be thoughtful about what type of partnership is used as part of their co-mentoring. Among the possibilities are the following.

Early Career Mentors Paired With Other Early Career Mentors

When experienced teachers become mentors, they face steep learning that includes building a new knowledge base about mentoring as well as potentially needing to learn about different grade-level bands, content areas, standards, instructional activities (IAs), and more! If they are mentoring in a new building or across multiple buildings, they need to understand each school's climate, culture, and priorities. They also need to build new relationships with teachers, students, administrators, and other school staff.

In addition to all of this change, moving out of the classroom can feel isolating, and many mentors mourn the loss of deep and sustained relationships with students. Partnering new mentors to work together toward shared or individual goals provides space for reflection, analysis, and action planning *and* can simultaneously alleviate isolation.

New mentors collaborating with one another might enact a problem-solving protocol in order to discuss challenges they are experiencing, practice a specific mentoring tool or practice together, or even go into classrooms together to calibrate their observational lenses. Providing mentors with specific protocols for each of these processes can help ensure that co-mentoring conversations are productive.

Early Career Mentors Paired With Veteran Mentors

Partnering early career and veteran mentors can have positive effects for both parties. Veteran mentors can draw upon their expertise to support newer colleagues to deepen their knowledge and responsiveness with enacting specific mentoring practices. For example, veterans can help new mentors prioritize what to selectively script during an observation or help them proactively work through the nuances of effective demonstration teaching (see Chapter 11). At the same time, a veteran mentor's experience facilitating their newer colleague's learning can deepen their own understanding of that mentoring practice.

While newer mentors have less mentoring expertise, they may have more familiarity with recently adopted learning standards or may have experience with an IA that the veteran does not. Furthermore, they may have had an abundance of informal mentor experience or even many years mentoring preservice teachers. Therefore, their potential contributions should not be underestimated.

Veteran Mentors Together

Similar to grouping new mentors, partnering mentors with multiple years of experience can alleviate isolation while also providing differentiated professional learning by capitalizing on their mutual expertise. Two or more veteran mentors might observe one another debriefing a teacher (see Chapter 4). As they observe they may collect data using slightly modified tools described in Chapter 3 and then engage in their own debrief, where they give each other goal-focused feedback. In another case, they may engage in co-planning to support one another in enacting less commonly used, but highly impactful, inside practices such as demonstration teaching and co-teaching (see Chapters 11 and 12).

Grade-Level or Content-Area Partnerships

At times, given programmatic or mentor-specific goals, it is more appropriate to partner mentors by grade-level or content-area expertise rather than considering experience levels. Mentors have grade-level and content expertise, but let's face it, no mentor taught all subjects across PK–12! In their transition to the role of mentor, they may well find themselves mentoring teachers across grade levels and content areas that do not reflect their expertise or experiences. Mentors, new and veteran alike, may benefit from co-mentoring with another mentor with different classroom experiences.

For example, a mentor who taught third and fifth grade, all subjects, could easily find themselves mentoring an eighth-grade math teacher. Partnering with a mentor who taught seventh-, eighth-, or ninth-grade math may provide much-needed perspective. In other cases, such as supporting teachers in curricular shifts like NGSS and NCSS, teams may want to strategically partner all mentors who support science or social studies teachers for targeted co-mentoring. In these ways co-mentoring can distribute expertise and responsibility for development.

Small Groups of Mixed-Background Mentors Sharing a Similar Goal

There may also be a time, during or after a team-wide PD or midyear reflection and goal setting, when a mentoring team wants to divide into small groups of two to five mentors and engage in co-mentoring as a way of applying and deepening their learning. For example, if the PD introduces a new data collection tool such as an IA checklist (see Chapter 3), small teams may go into preselected classrooms (with teacher approval, of course), to try out and compare notes about the tool. This grouping is effective for any data collection tool or mentoring practice.

SETTING THE STAGE FOR EFFECTIVE CO-MENTORING

Co-mentoring, like nearly all mentoring practices, begins with a *prebrief*, where a *focus is set*. In setting a focus, mentors may find it helpful to use (a) goals set at the beginning and throughout the year; (b) feedback received from peers and supervisors; (c) needs they have identified based on a specific interaction(s) with their teachers; and/or (d) programmatic or team goals/needs established by the team director. Some common focus areas include

- a specific, challenging mentoring practice or aspect of that practice;
- improving interactions with a specific teacher; and
- expanding or deepening their repertoire of mentoring practices and data observation tools.

Then, given the focus, mentors must *determine what combination of inside/ outside practices makes sense to help better understand that focus*. Mentors should draw from the full set of inside/outside practices that they use with teachers and adapt them to benefit co-mentors. Some possible examples include

- co-observe and co-collect data using a predetermined tool;
- step in during a colleague's debrief, demonstration or co-teaching, a rehearsal, and so forth;
- demonstrate or rehearse an upcoming debrief, co-planning session, demonstration, or cotaught lesson;
- co-debrief with a teacher in largely predetermined ways, particularly useful when a mentor is working with a teacher in an area beyond their expertise (e.g., grade level, content, IA); and
- briefly touch base in-person or virtually for quick problem solving, to give and receive updates, and to provide support, mirroring the brief interactions used with teachers (see Chapter 5).

Regardless of which practice(s) co-mentors draw upon in their collaborations, to maximize impact, they must d*ebrief the co-mentored experience*. Because combinations of co-mentoring are so variable, debriefing may come *after* another practice such as co-observation of a teacher or observation of a mentor-teacher debrief. Or the debrief may be *part of* another practice, such as co-planning or rehearsals. Whenever the debrief occurs, it is critical that mentors ask and answer, related to the mentoring focus:

> "What's working/What worked? What did we see related to the focus that was effective? What made X work/effective?" It is always important that mentors take time to reflect on strengths/successes of their own and each other's practice. This is especially true in co-mentoring. No matter the practices used in co-mentoring, *both* mentors have a chance to come together to learn from and offer targeted feedback and support to one another.

> "As we reflect on [focus practice], what is still challenging? What is contributing to these challenges?" Co-mentoring brings together two individuals with at least some shared knowledge of practice, which allows for a more targeted analysis of challenges!

> "Based on the co-mentoring experience, what meaningful changes can I/ we make to my/our practice? What are meaningful next steps I/we can take to improve my/our practice? What support do I/we need and from where can I/we get it?" Now that the areas of growth have been identified and analyzed, *next steps* must be generated to facilitate improvement in that area. This will likely include drawing from some combination of the mentor-adapted inside and outside practices. Importantly, mentors spend so much time thinking about and supporting their teachers that decision fatigue can happen. Having a trusted colleague co-think about actionable next steps *and* know that follow-up will occur can help mentors dedicate the time and space to work on their own professional needs.

PROACTIVELY ADDRESSING POTENTIAL CONCERNS

Programs/individual mentors may hesitate to engage in co-mentoring because it is time consuming. Without proper preparation and support for each mentor, it could also result in non-best practices being perpetuated. The issue of time can be addressed by building co-mentoring into existing professional development structures. For example, in lieu of a half- or full-day professional development (PD) program, mentors instead break into small groups or partners and co-mentor! Where this is not possible, because of its capacity to improve the quality of mentoring and therefore outcomes for teachers, co-mentoring may be incorporated into existing mentoring expectations.

Concerns about mentor preparation and support can be addressed in a range of ways, including, thoughtful, well-designed protocols and data collection tools that are taught and modeled during initial and ongoing training. Additionally, programs that engage in well-designed and ongoing PD (see Chapter 13 and Appendix C) and mentor development sessions (see Chapter 16) have built-in models for what co-mentoring can and should address and look like. Finally, providing mentors with clearly defined expectations against which to measure their practices can further increase the likelihood that co-mentoring perpetuates best practices.

FINAL THOUGHTS ON CO-MENTORING

Co-mentoring provides opportunities to learn with and from each other. Co-mentoring reduces the isolation that mentors frequently experience after they transition from the classroom, making it worth the time and effort required. Co-mentoring can be a way for mentors to help each other refine and calibrate their respective lenses on teaching and learning, how they work with new teachers, and their own effectiveness. Co-mentoring also helps an individual mentor go beyond their own perspectives and knowledge base and provide insights that are more comprehensive than what a mentor could do own their own. Additionally, through co-mentoring, mentors become a network of support, ready to respond with feedback, strategies, examples, resources, suggestions, and when needed, encouragement!

QUESTIONS FOR REFLECTION AND ACTION

1. Have you ever co-mentored with a colleague, formally or informally? Which practices did you use (See "Setting the Stage for Effective Co-mentoring" for some ideas)? What went well? What were the challenges? What other ideas or recommendations for co-mentoring do you have?

2. If you have not co-mentored, how might the information in this chapter help you weave co-mentoring into your repertoire? Are there specific parts of your mentoring practice where co-mentoring might be beneficial? Are there specific co-mentoring practices you would like to try? Who might be a colleague that you could co-mentor with?

3. When you consider co-mentoring, what is your initial reaction? Are there things that you find exciting about this practice? Things that make you uncertain or uncomfortable? With whom might you co-mentor? If you mentor separate from a team or program, how might you find virtual co-mentors?

Chapter Sixteen

Mentor Development Sessions

Learning With and From Team Leaders

As a new mentor I also think that you need to have professional development, but you need more, you know? My manager Ruby helps me not just reflect but also pushes my practice, gives me an extra set of eyes on my practice to help me identify what's most important. I have 1:1 time with her where I can be observed and get immediate feedback, where I can see her model for me, where she listens and answers my questions. It's almost like having my own mentor.—Lacey, first-year mentor

Educative mentoring is a collaborative, responsive, scaffolded, and situated framework (i.e., it occurs in the teacher's daily teaching context) aimed at fostering teachers' professional learning. The principles that inform educative mentoring for teachers are also impactful for fostering mentors' professional growth. Much in the same way that teachers benefit from the skilled support of mentors, mentors also benefit from the opportunity to experience flexible and differentiated support from more experienced and knowledgeable mentors.

Mentor development sessions (MDSs) align with an educative stance. MDSs are particularly impactful for helping mentors translate principles and strategies of educative mentoring into an effective mentoring practice. In an MDS, a program *lead* (typically a director, manager, school leader, or experienced mentor with a track record of success) takes on the role of the mentor, while the *mentor* takes on the role of mentee. Together they engage in cycles of inquiry modeled after the mentoring cycles used with teachers.

SETTING THE STAGE FOR AN EFFECTIVE MDS

Unlike co-mentoring, where the mentors involved collaborate intentionally to facilitate growth among themselves, in an MDS, the goal is for the *lead* to facilitate growth in the mentor. Therefore, it is critical that the lead has demonstrated effectiveness, deep knowledge, and the ability to implement the principles and practices of educative mentoring. MDSs are most effective when they are an integrated and consistent component of mentors' professional development (PD). Though, just as educative mentoring must be responsive, MDSs may also be used in a more impromptu fashion, being scheduled in response to a specific need or challenge.

Setting Goals

Through the MDS, mentor and lead collaborate through a process similar to the mentoring cycle described in this book. The MDS cycle should begin with a prebrief that allows mentor and lead to establish a focus for the session. The focus for an MDS may be based on

- beginning-of-the-year goals;
- fine-tuning prior goals based on progress and reflection;
- feedback mentors have received from peers, supervisors, and/or their teachers;
- emerging needs stemming from interaction(s) with teachers;
- programmatic, school, or district initiatives;
- team goals; and
- goals the lead suggests or that are determined through joint problem solving.

The Lead Supports Mentors' Progress Toward Goal

Based on the mentor's goals, the lead and mentor should determine which combination of inside/outside practices, drawing from the full compendium available, is most appropriate to understand and ultimately address their focus for improvement. Whatever the methods selected, it is critical to

- align the MDS focus with the mentor's goal(s);
- allocate sufficient time for lead and mentor to engage in in-depth analysis and problem solving; and
- identify next steps for both lead and mentor to support successful implementation of the work explored via the MDS.

Depending on mentors' experience, expertise, and current caseloads, there can be any number of foci. Leads and mentors should problem-solve to identify top priorities. What follows are examples of frequently requested, high-impact MDS foci

Caseload Review

Lead and mentor talk through each teacher that the mentor is supporting and

- discuss long-term goals and progress toward goals;
- identify and trouble-shoot challenges; and
- brainstorm next steps and specific mentoring practices to support each teacher.

Trouble-Shooting a Challenging Case

Especially in the case of an impromptu MDS, mentors may want support addressing a situation with a teacher or administrator, such as

- working with a teacher who appears disengaged from their mentor,
- working with a teacher who appears resistant to setting goals or following through with next steps,
- supporting a teacher with low expectations for students,
- repairing a relationship that has been damaged, and
- navigating tensions between teachers and administrators.

Co-observation in One or More Classrooms

Lead and mentor co-observe, co-collect data, co-plan for, and/or co-debrief in order to

- calibrate lenses to evaluate whether both are finding similar areas of strength and need;
- calibrate data collection practices to ensure that, given the same tool, both find similar patterns of data;
- expand data collection tool use; and
- identify potential foci for subsequent mentoring cycles with a teacher.

Demonstrate and/or Rehearse

Demonstrate (outside) and/or rehearse (see Chapter 9) to build mentor knowledge and skill. Leads may demonstrate or facilitate the rehearsal of any mentoring practice or data collection tool usage one-on-one with the mentor or with the mentor and a teacher.

Co-planning and Preparing for a Debrief

Reviewing data, planning for, and facilitating effective debriefs require a great deal of knowledge, skill, and responsiveness. Leads may

- help mentors organize and prepare data;
- evaluate which language stems they might use, questions they might ask, IAs they might demonstrate/rehearse, and so forth;
- determine potential next steps for one or more of their teachers; and
- demonstrate and/or rehearse areas of need.

Analyzing Video

Lead and mentor may view video footage of the mentor debriefing, co-teaching, demonstration teaching, or nearly any other mentoring practice (see Chapter 14).

MDSs, like educative mentoring with teachers, have a seemingly endless combination of practices that, if used with intentionality and accompanied by meaningful discussion, can make a direct and observable impact on mentors' practice.

PROACTIVELY ADDRESSING POTENTIAL CONCERNS

First, MDSs are learning opportunities. Some mentors may embrace the opportunity for one-on-one support from an experienced mentor. Yet, some other mentors may feel insecure or vulnerable. After all, MDSs put a mentor's own practice front and center.

When engaging in an MDS, a lead may directly observe a mentor collecting data or facilitating a debrief, have the mentor rehearse a specific practice, or co-analyze video of a mentor's practice. In any of these examples mentors may worry that misconceptions, gaps in practice, and mistakes will become visible to themselves and their lead. Mutual trust and clear procedures, structures, and purposes for any of the practices leads and mentors engage in (i.e., "a safe space to try something out with support") can mitigate these concerns.

In a similar vein, leads may find themselves in a more vulnerable position when demonstrating a practice or an IA, particularly when they are doing so with a teacher. They may worry about the demonstration not going well, particularly if they have a limited relationship with the teacher. Or conversely, the lead may worry that it will go too well and the mentor may feel inadequate in their own skills.

As always, relationships, trust, clear expectations, a humble spirit, and a willingness to analyze and learn from "failures" and successes alike mitigate some of the concern. Furthermore, any "successful" or "challenging" experience that a lead has with a mentor and/or teacher is an opportunity to model reflection and a genuine desire to constantly grow. After all, even "successful" teaching and learning experiences should include "next steps" for further growth.

MDSs require leads to invest sustained and significant time in supporting their mentors. Scheduling time can be challenging due to busy schedules, when leads and mentors are in different buildings, and any number of other reasons. Based on lead and mentor needs, MDSs can be in-person or virtual, through the use of video technology, live-streaming, or file-share programs (e.g., Dropbox and Google Drive).

Even with a deep desire to support all mentors on a team, that may not always be possible. Leads may address this by building MDSs into their existing schedules and frameworks for professional development. Leads might differentiate the frequency of support for new versus veteran mentors (e.g., biweekly versus monthly).

Additionally, leads may find that delegating at least some responsibility for MDSs to more experienced and skilled mentors alleviates some of the demands. For example, the team lead may select two or three of their experienced, top-performing mentors and ask each of them to engage in regular MDSs with one or two new/early career mentors. Doing so could be career development, preparing these skilled and experienced mentors to transition to program leads or other leadership roles if they so choose.

FINAL THOUGHTS ON MDSS

Through goal setting, facilitated reflection, and incorporating many of the same mentoring practices and processes mentors use with teachers, the MDS structure provides differentiated, contextualized, and scaffolded development. MDSs situate mentors as learners and have them experience the same processes and practices that they implement with their teachers. Experiencing practices such as demonstrations and co-debriefing not only helps mentors move closer toward their goals but also can provide an image of skilled practice that they can draw upon in their work with teachers. In this manner, MDSs provide mentors with highly personalized support that can increase their efficacy, confidence, willingness, and ability to draw from the full range of inside/outside practices to facilitate teachers' professional growth.

QUESTIONS FOR REFLECTION AND ACTION

1. Have you ever used facilitated or participated in an MDS? What went well? What were the challenges? Which practice(s) were used as part of the MDS? Were they effective? How do you know?

2. When you consider MDSs, through your own experiences, or considering them for future practice, what is your initial reaction? Are there things you find exciting about this practice? Things that make you uncertain or uncomfortable?

3. Think back upon/reflect forward to your work mentoring teachers. Do you see opportunities where MDSs could have been/would be beneficial to your confidence and/or mentoring practice? What might this have looked like/look like?

4. How might the information in this chapter help you weave MDSs into your repertoire or program supports? What would it take for this implementation to happen?

5. If MDSs are or have been in your repertoire, are there any insights from this chapter that could help you augment or fine-tune what you are already doing? What, from your own practice, might augment or extend the information provided in this chapter?

Afterword

Final Thoughts as You Move Forward With Educative Mentoring

Every child deserves an excellent teacher. Excellent teachers are made, not born. Mentoring is an impactful process that can help teachers reach their fullest potential.

We believe in the power and promise of mentoring. We believe that responsive mentors who enact educative mentoring principles and practices will not only promote job satisfaction and retention for their teachers but also ensure their teachers are able to implement ambitious instruction, thereby ensuring *all* students receive the type of expansive education that builds positive academic identities and expands their life opportunities. We hope this book, its framing, and the mentoring practices described give you even more ways to collaborate with, support, and build capacity in your teachers.

We also know that good mentors are made, not born. Even highly successful teachers face a steep learning curve as they transition over to the role of mentor. We want to empower mentors and teachers to set ambitious instructional goals with the firm belief that mentors should have a repertoire of responsive practices to help them achieve their aims. Setting ambitious goals requires risk. Educative mentors know how to facilitate collaborative, scaffolded, contextualized, teacher-centered learning that fosters ambitious teaching and learning. We hope the mentor-the-mentor section provides you with ways to support your own and your colleagues' growth.

Some ideas and practices described in this book may be new. Others may build upon what you already know and do. We hope that the sum of this book helps you mentor in even more responsive and skilled ways. We thank you for engaging with us in this work, and we wish you the best as you move forward and continue to make a significant and sustained impact on the lives of teachers and students alike.

Appendix A

Data Collection Tools

SELECTIVE SCRIPTING TEMPLATES

Selective Scripting (3-Column) Template

Teacher: _____ Date: _____

Mentor: _____ Grade Level: _____

Observation Focus: _____

Time Stamps/ Lesson Portion	Teacher Words/Actions	Student Words/ Actions	Coach Notes/ Observations

Selective Scripting (2-Column) Template

Teacher: _____ Date: _____

Mentor: _____ Grade Level: _____

Observation Focus: _____

Time Stamps/ Lesson Portion	Teacher Word/Actions	Student Word/Actions

SEATING CHART EXAMPLES

Because each seating chart will be individualized to the observed-teacher's classroom, two examples are provided—there are dozens of other mentoring focuses that seating charts can support, using nearly unlimited coding options.

Example A reflects data collected in real time, each time a target event happens.

Example A:

M R	M R/+
F R R R/	F

F R R/+	M
F	F R R R R

F R R R R R R	M R
NO ONE	F

F R R	M R/+
M	F

F T T	NO ONE
M TD T	M OD OD OD

F	M R R R/+
F	F R R R

Example A Key to Codes:

M=Male	*F = Female*	*O= Out of seat*	*D=Redirected by teacher*
R=Raises hand	*/=Called on*	*+ = Correct answer*	*T= Talks out of turn*

Seating chart example

Example Debriefing Questions

- What, if any, patterns do you notice regarding who is/is not volunteering to respond (i.e., raising their hands)? Given that, what could you try differently in subsequent lessons to support more robust participation?
- What, if any, patterns do you notice regarding who is called upon? Given that, what could you try differently in subsequent lessons to ensure more robust participation?

Example B reflects a "scan and record" option: every x minutes, mentors scan the room and record data for each student at that given period of time.

C	C	C	C	C	C	C	C
			C				C
N	N	C	C	N	N	N	C
C	C	C	C	C	C	C	C
			N				C
C	C	N	N	C	C	N	N

C	C	C	C	C	C	C	C
			C				C
C	C	N	C	C	N	N	C
C	C	C	C	C	C	C	N
			C				C
C	C	C	C	C	C	N	N

C	C	C	C	N	C	N	N
			C				C
C	C	N	C	C	C	N	C
C	C	C	C	C	C	N	N
			C				C
C	C	C	C	C	C	N	C

C	C	C	C	C	C	C	C
			C				C
C	N	N	C	C	C	N	C
C	C	C	C	C	C	C	C
			C				C
C	C	C	C	N	C	N	C

Example B Key to Codes:

C–Completing the teacher-assigned task

N–Not currently completing the teacher-assigned task

Example B Time Stamps when the classroom

was scanned and data collected:

10:10	10:12	10:14	10:16
			10:18
10:26	10:24	10:22	10:20

Seating chart example: "scan and record" option

Example Debriefing Questions

- What, if any, patterns do you notice regarding when in the lesson students are most likely off task? What is happening during instruction at these times? What could be contributing to these higher rates of off-task behavior?
- What, if any, patterns do you notice regarding who is most likely to be off task? What is happening during instruction at these times? What could be contributing to these higher rates of off-task behavior?

Appendix A

CHECKLIST EXAMPLE

Focus: Facilitating Whole-Group Discussions

Criteria	Observed	Not Observed	Notes

Discussion is framed by
- Communicating a purpose for discussion to students
- Making expectations for student participation explicit
- Answering student questions
- Providing/reviewing background readings, data, or other resources needed for meaningful discussion

Discussion is initiated by
- Providing a clear, open-ended prompt with multiple potential student responses to the class verbally and written

Discussion is facilitated by
- Having students discuss with a partner or write responses prior to sharing with the whole class
- Ensuring wait time
- Occasionally interjecting a follow-up prompt if the conversation stalls or follows a tangent

Discussion is closed by
- Summarizing key points made
- Providing students with space to share their final thoughts, verbal, written, or otherwise

Other notes:

Appendix B

Brief Interaction | Template and Example

HELLO   Teacher: _____   Date: _____

          Mentor: _____   Grade Level: _____

I stopped in today to _____

While I was here, I noticed …

Ideas…

                                                                    Thanks!

HELLO   Teacher: _____   Date: _____

          Mentor: _____   Grade Level: _____

I stopped in today to _____

Brief interaction template

BRIEF INTERACTION EXAMPLE

While I was here, I noticed . . .

- Your directions were clear and concise and you showed them a visual (poster), setting students up for success.
- Your use of a lamp, rug, plants, motivational quotes, high school materials, and group seating set a "homey" feeling that will help build a sense of safety for your students.

Ideas . . .

- It might be helpful to teach and practice a standard procedure for handing out and collecting materials—will save valuable instructional time.
- I'll stop by to check in with you and set up a time to meet later this week! Don't hesitate to call/text (123-456-7890) or email (flast@mentoremail.org) with any questions or concerns!

                                                                    Thanks!

Appendix C

Suggested Mentor Professional Development Topics, Timelines, and Resources

NEW MENTORS—BEFORE THE SCHOOL YEAR STARTS

Topic	*Recommended Resources*
Principles of Educative Mentoring	• Chapter 1 of this book • Feiman-Nemser, S. (1998). Teachers as teacher educators. *European Journal of Teacher Education, 21,* 63–74. • Feiman-Nemser, S. (2001). From preparation to practice: Designing a continuum to strengthen and sustain teaching. *Teachers College Record, 103*(6), 1013–1055. • Feiman-Nemser, S. (2012). *Teachers as learners.* Cambridge, MA: Harvard Educational Press.
Programmatic Expectations and Mentoring Standards	• From the New Teacher Center: http://info.newteachercenter.org/l/576393/2018-08-14/346x78b. • Appendix D in Aguilar, E. (2013). *The art of coaching: Effective strategies for school transformation.* San Francisco, CA: Jossey-Bass.
Principles of Adult Learning	• Chapter 8 in Sweeney, D. (2011). *Student-centered coaching: Coaches and principals.* Thousand Oaks, CA: Corwin Press. • IRIS Module: "How People Learn: Presenting the Learning Theory and Inquiry Cycle on Which the IRIS Modules Are Built," https://iris.peabody.vanderbilt.edu/module/hpl.
Introduction to Inside/Outside Practices	• Chapter 1 of this book • Gardiner, W., & Weisling, N. F. (2018). Challenges and complexities of building a mentoring practice: Insights from new mentors. *International Journal of Mentoring and Coaching in Education, 7*(4), 329–342. • Schwille, S. A. (2008). The professional practice of mentoring. *American Journal of Education, 115,* 139–167.
Building Relationships	• Chapter 2 of this book • Chapter 5 in Aguilar, E. (2013). *The art of coaching: Effective strategies for school transformation.* San Francisco, CA: Jossey-Bass. • Chapter 2 in Sweeney, D. (2011). *Student-centered coaching: Coaches and principals.* Thousand Oaks, CA: Corwin Press.
Initial Mentoring Practices	• Chapters 3–5 in this book • For instructive, collaborative, and facilitative language stems as well as examples of tools from the New Teacher Center: Chapter 3 in Moir, E., Barlin, D., Gless, J., & Miles, J. (2009). *New teacher mentoring: Hopes and promise for improving teacher effectiveness.* Cambridge, MA: Harvard Education Press.

- Language stances: Chapter 4 in Achinstein, B., & Athanases, S. Z. (2006). *Mentors in the making: Developing new leaders for new teachers*. New York, NY: Teachers College Press.
- Listening, questioning, and facilitating conversations: Chapters 8–12 in Aguilar, E. (2013). *The art of coaching: Effective strategies for school transformation*. San Francisco, CA: Jossey-Bass.
- Data: Chapter 4 in Sweeney, D. (2011). *Student-centered coaching: Coaches and principals*. Thousand Oaks, CA: Corwin Press.

RETURNING MENTORS—BEFORE THE SCHOOL YEAR STARTS

Topic	Recommended Resources
Reflecting on previous practice (using program standards and feedback from teachers, administrators, and/or program leads/directors, etc.)	• Mentoring standards from the New Teacher Center: http://info.newteachercenter.org/l/576393/2018-08-14/346x78b. • Appendix D in Aguilar, E. (2013). *The art of coaching: Effective strategies for school transformation*. San Francisco, CA: Jossey-Bass. • A simple internet search of "mentor feedback forms" yields a wide range of results that can be adapted for a specific mentoring context.
Goal setting	• Chapter 13 in this book

ADDITIONAL PD TOPICS

Here are additional professional development (PD) topics for all mentors across the school year (using PD structures as well as video analysis, co-mentoring, and MDSs as appropriate):

- Introduction/deeper dive into specific mentoring practices
- PD on disciplinary standards (e.g., CCSS, NCSS, NGSS)
- Unique challenges of supporting specialist teachers (e.g., art, physical education) and special educators (inclusive, resource, and/or self-contained)
- Culturally responsive and sustaining classroom practices
- Mentoring for equity
- Rigorous instruction
- Ambitious instructional activities
- Reflecting on teachers' progress

References

Aguilar, E. (2013). *The art of coaching: Effective strategies for school transformation.* San Francisco, CA: Jossey-Bass.

Aspfors, J., & Fransson, G. (2015). Research on mentor education for mentors of newly qualified teachers: A qualitative meta-synthesis. *Teaching and Teacher Education, 48,* 75–86.

Berliner, D. (2001). Learning about and learning from expert teachers. *International Journal of Educational Research, 35,* 463–482.

Bloom, G., Castagna, C., Moir, E., & Warren, B. (2005). *Blended coaching: Skills and strategies to support principal development.* Thousand Oaks, CA: Corwin Press.

Britzman, D. (2003). *Practice makes practice: A critical study of learning to teach.* Albany, NY: State University of New York Press.

Cazden, C. (2001). *Classroom discourse: The language of teaching and learning* (2nd ed.). Portsmouth, NH: Heinemann.

City, E. A., Elmore, R. F., Fiarman, S. E., & Teitel, E. (2009). *Instructional rounds in education: A network approach to improving teaching and learning.* Cambridge, MA: Harvard Education Press.

Feiman-Nemser, S. (1998). Teachers as teacher educators. *European Journal of Teacher Education, 21,* 63–74.

Feiman-Nemser, S. (2001). From preparation to practice: Designing a continuum to strengthen and sustain teaching. *Teachers College Record, 103*(6), 1013–1055.

Feiman-Nemser, S. (2012). *Teachers as learners.* Cambridge, MA: Harvard Educational Press.

Friend, M., & Cook, L. (2016). *Interactions: Collaboration skills for school professionals* (8th ed). New York, NY: Merrill.

Gardiner, W. (2017). Mentoring "inside" and "outside" the action of teaching: A professional framework for mentoring. *The New Educator, 13*(1), 53–71.

Gardiner, W. (2019). Rehearsals in clinical placements: Scaffolding teacher candidates' literacy instruction. *The Teacher Educator, 53*(4), 384–400.

Gardiner, W., & Weisling, N. F. (2016). Mentoring "inside" the action of teaching: Induction coaches' perspectives and practices. *Professional Development in Education, 42*(5), 671–686.

Gardiner, W., & Weisling, N. F. (2018). Challenges and complexities of building a mentoring practice: Insights from new mentors. *International Journal of Mentoring and Coaching in Education, 7*(4), 329–342.

Gay, G. (2018). *Culturally responsive teaching: Theory, research and practice* (3rd ed.). New York: Teachers College Press.

Grossman, P., Compton, C., Igra, D., Ronfeldt, M., Shahan, E., & Williamson, P. (2009). Teaching practice: A cross-professional perspective. *Teachers College Record, 111,* 2055–2100.

Gurarino, C., Santibañez, L., & Daley, C. (2006). Teacher recruitment and retention: A review of the recent empirical literature. *Review of Research in Education, 76*(2), 173–208.

Ingersoll, R. M., Merrill, E., Stuckey, D., & Collins, G. (2018). Seven trends: The transformation of the teaching force. Updated October 2018. CPRE Research Reports . Retrieved from https://repository.upenn.edu/cpre_researchreports/108

Ingersoll, R. M. & Strong, M. (2011). The impact of induction and mentoring programs for beginning teachers: A critical review of the research. *Review of Educational Research, 81*(2), 201–233.

Jackson, P. (1990). *Life in classrooms*. New York, NY: Teachers College Press.

Ladson-Billings, G. (2014). Culturally relevant teaching 2.0: A.k.a. the remix. *Teachers College Record, 84*(1), 74–84.

Moll, L. C., Amati, C., Neff, D., & Gomez, N. (1992). Funds of knowledge for teaching: Using a qualitative approach to connect homes and classrooms. *Theory Into Practice, 31(2),* 132–141.

Paris, D. (2012). Culturally sustaining pedagogy: A needed change in stance, terminology, and pedagogy. *Educational Researcher, 41*(3), 93–97.

Schwille, S. A. (2008). The professional practice of mentoring. *American Journal of Education, 115,* 139–167.

Simon, N. S., & Moore-Johnson, S. (2015). Teacher turnover in high-poverty schools: What we know and can do. *Teachers College Record, 117*(3), 1–36.

Wang, J., & Odell, S. J. (2002). Mentored learning to teach according to standards-based reform: A critical review. *Review of Educational Research, 72,* 481–546.

About the Authors

Wendy Gardiner is Jolita Hylland Benson Endowed Chair in Elementary Education and associate professor at Pacific Lutheran University where she teaches literacy methods courses and multicultural children's literature. Her research interests include educative mentoring and teacher education in literacy. She began her career teaching grades K–3 in Chicago Public Schools.

Nina F. Weisling is assistant professor of education at Carthage College in Kenosha, Wisconsin, where she primarily teaches courses related to special education and conducts research related to mentoring and inclusive practices. Prior to this she was a special educator, general educator, and mentor for preservice, new, and veteran teachers.

Made in the USA
Las Vegas, NV
06 October 2021